# THIS PLANNER
## BELONGS TO

**SCHOOL** | **ROOM**

**GRADE**

**ADDRESS**

**EMAIL**

**PHONE**

# CONTACTS & VOLUNTEERS

| NAME | CONTACT INFO |
|------|--------------|
|      |              |

# Welcome

## SCHEDULE

SCHOOL BEGINS: _____

LUNCH: _____

RECESS: _____

SPECIALS: _____

SCHOOL ENDS: _____

_____

## NEED HELP?

**RELIABLE STUDENTS:** _____

_____

_____

**TEACHERS:** _____

_____

_____

**PRINCIPAL:** _____

_____

**VICE PRINCIPAL:** _____

_____

**OTHER STAFF:** _____

_____

_____

## SPECIAL SCHEDULES

| NAMES | TIME | LOCATION |
|-------|------|----------|
| _____ | _____ |
| _____ | _____ |
| _____ | _____ |
| _____ | _____ |
| _____ | _____ |
| _____ | _____ |

## ADDITIONAL NOTES

_____

_____

_____

_____

_____

_____

# COMMUNICATION LOG

| DATE | TYPE | NAME | PURPOSE | NOTES |
|------|------|------|---------|-------|
|  | 📱 @ 📄 👥 |  |  |  |
|  | 📱 @ 📄 👥 |  |  |  |
|  | 📱 @ 📄 👥 |  |  |  |
|  | 📱 @ 📄 👥 |  |  |  |
|  | 📱 @ 📄 👥 |  |  |  |
|  | 📱 @ 📄 👥 |  |  |  |
|  | 📱 @ 📄 👥 |  |  |  |
|  | 📱 @ 📄 👥 |  |  |  |
|  | 📱 @ 📄 👥 |  |  |  |
|  | 📱 @ 📄 👥 |  |  |  |
|  | 📱 @ 📄 👥 |  |  |  |
|  | 📱 @ 📄 👥 |  |  |  |
|  | 📱 @ 📄 👥 |  |  |  |
|  | 📱 @ 📄 👥 |  |  |  |
|  | 📱 @ 📄 👥 |  |  |  |
|  | 📱 @ 📄 👥 |  |  |  |
|  | 📱 @ 📄 👥 |  |  |  |
|  | 📱 @ 📄 👥 |  |  |  |
|  | 📱 @ 📄 👥 |  |  |  |
|  | 📱 @ 📄 👥 |  |  |  |
|  | 📱 @ 📄 👥 |  |  |  |
|  | 📱 @ 📄 👥 |  |  |  |
|  | 📱 @ 📄 👥 |  |  |  |
|  | 📱 @ 📄 👥 |  |  |  |
|  | 📱 @ 📄 👥 |  |  |  |
|  | 📱 @ 📄 👥 |  |  |  |
|  | 📱 @ 📄 👥 |  |  |  |

# COMMUNICATION LOG

| DATE | TYPE | NAME | PURPOSE | NOTES |
|---|---|---|---|---|
| | 📱 @ 📄 👥 | | | |
| | 📱 @ 📄 👥 | | | |
| | 📱 @ 📄 👥 | | | |
| | 📱 @ 📄 👥 | | | |
| | 📱 @ 📄 👥 | | | |
| | 📱 @ 📄 👥 | | | |
| | 📱 @ 📄 👥 | | | |
| | 📱 @ 📄 👥 | | | |
| | 📱 @ 📄 👥 | | | |
| | 📱 @ 📄 👥 | | | |
| | 📱 @ 📄 👥 | | | |
| | 📱 @ 📄 👥 | | | |
| | 📱 @ 📄 👥 | | | |
| | 📱 @ 📄 👥 | | | |
| | 📱 @ 📄 👥 | | | |
| | 📱 @ 📄 👥 | | | |
| | 📱 @ 📄 👥 | | | |
| | 📱 @ 📄 👥 | | | |
| | 📱 @ 📄 👥 | | | |
| | 📱 @ 📄 👥 | | | |
| | 📱 @ 📄 👥 | | | |
| | 📱 @ 📄 👥 | | | |
| | 📱 @ 📄 👥 | | | |
| | 📱 @ 📄 👥 | | | |
| | 📱 @ 📄 👥 | | | |
| | 📱 @ 📄 👥 | | | |
| | 📱 @ 📄 👥 | | | |

# NEWS AND NOTES

# NEWS AND NOTES

# PLAN IT

USE THESE PAGES TO CREATE A CLASSROOM PLAN, RECORD SEATING CHARTS, CREATE CHECKLISTS, SKETCH PLANS, ETC. THE OPTIONS ARE ENDLESS!

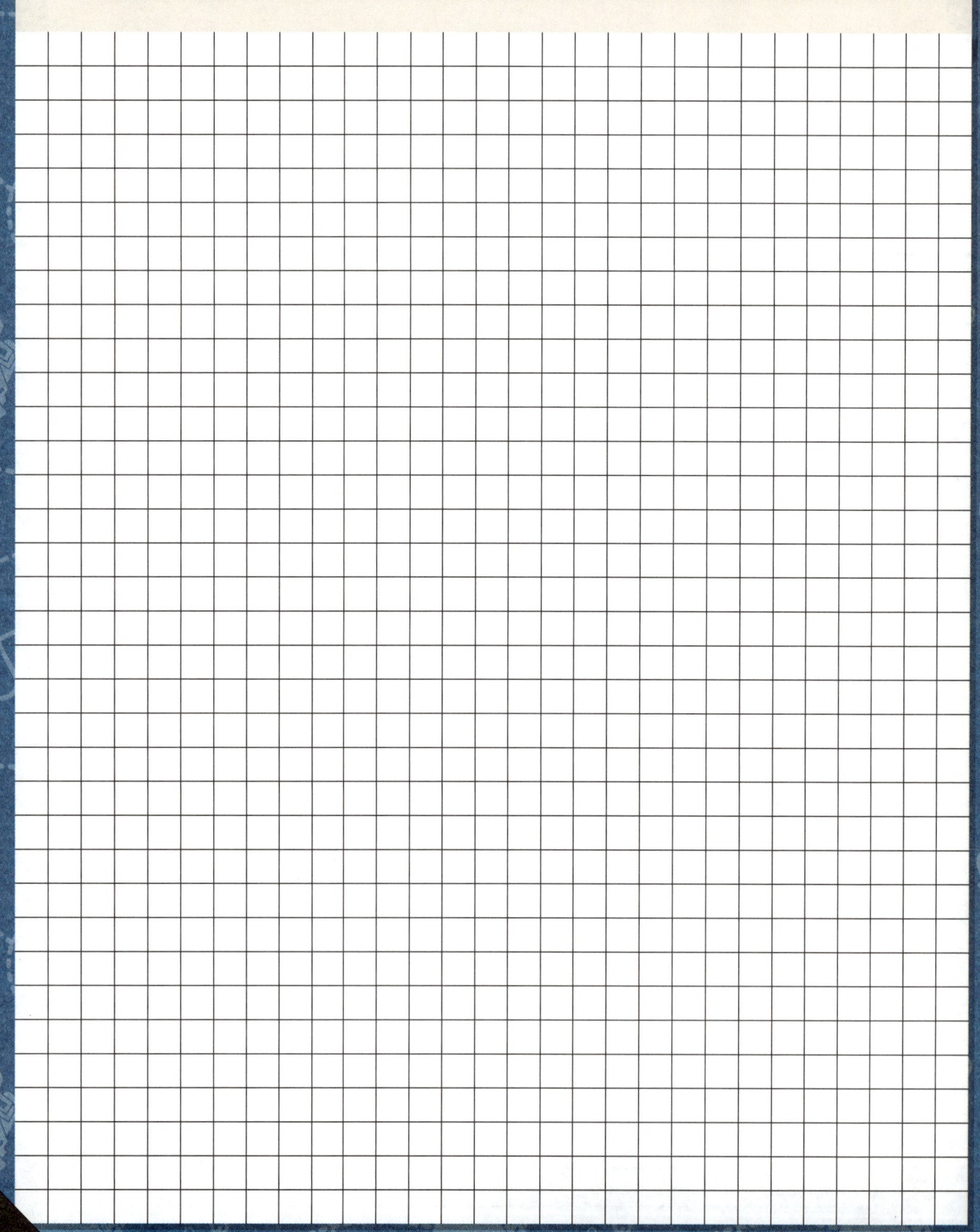

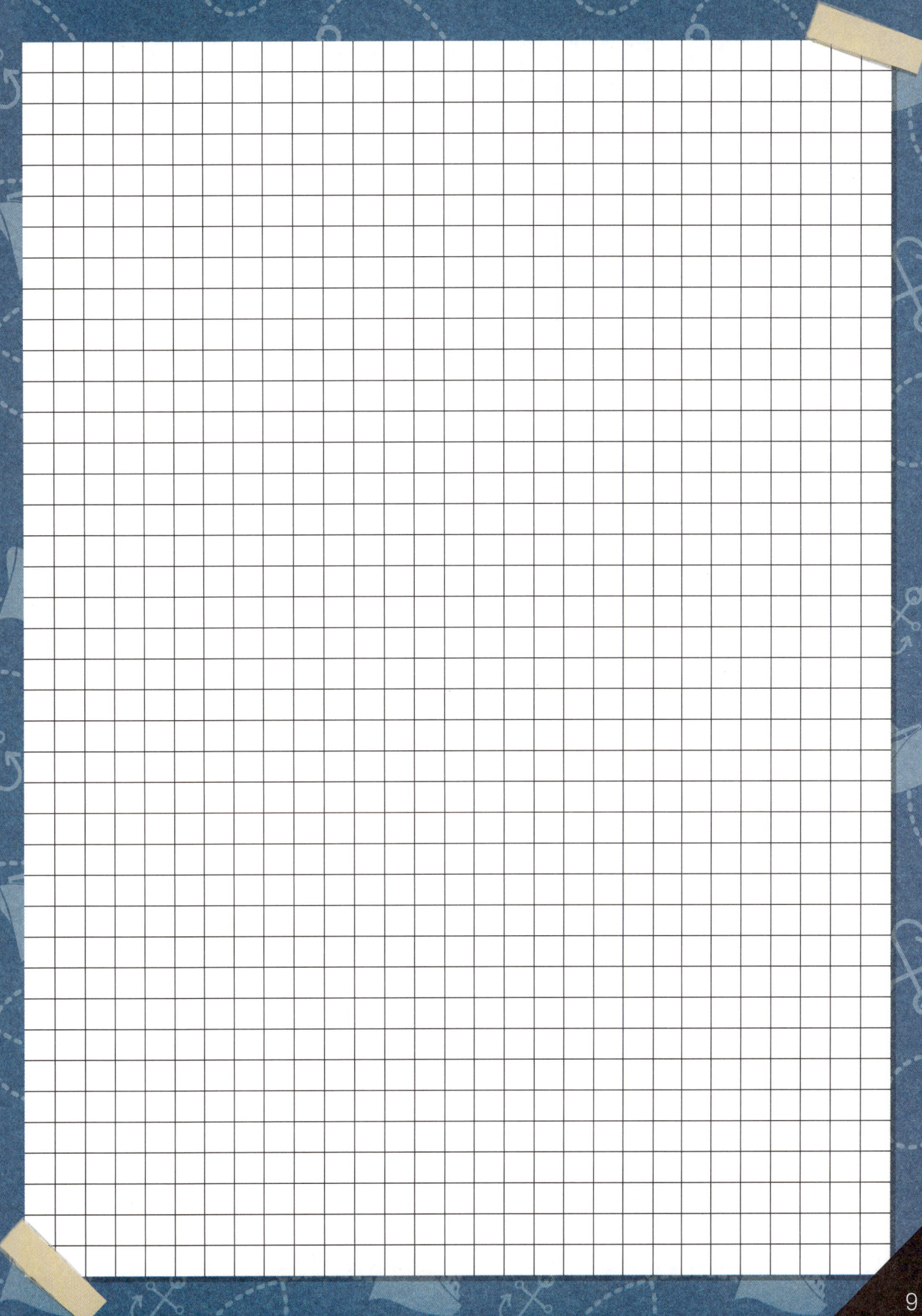

# YEAR AT A GLANCE

BON VOYAGE

**JULY**

**AUGUST**

**SEPTEMBER**

**OCTOBER**

**NOVEMBER**

**DECEMBER**

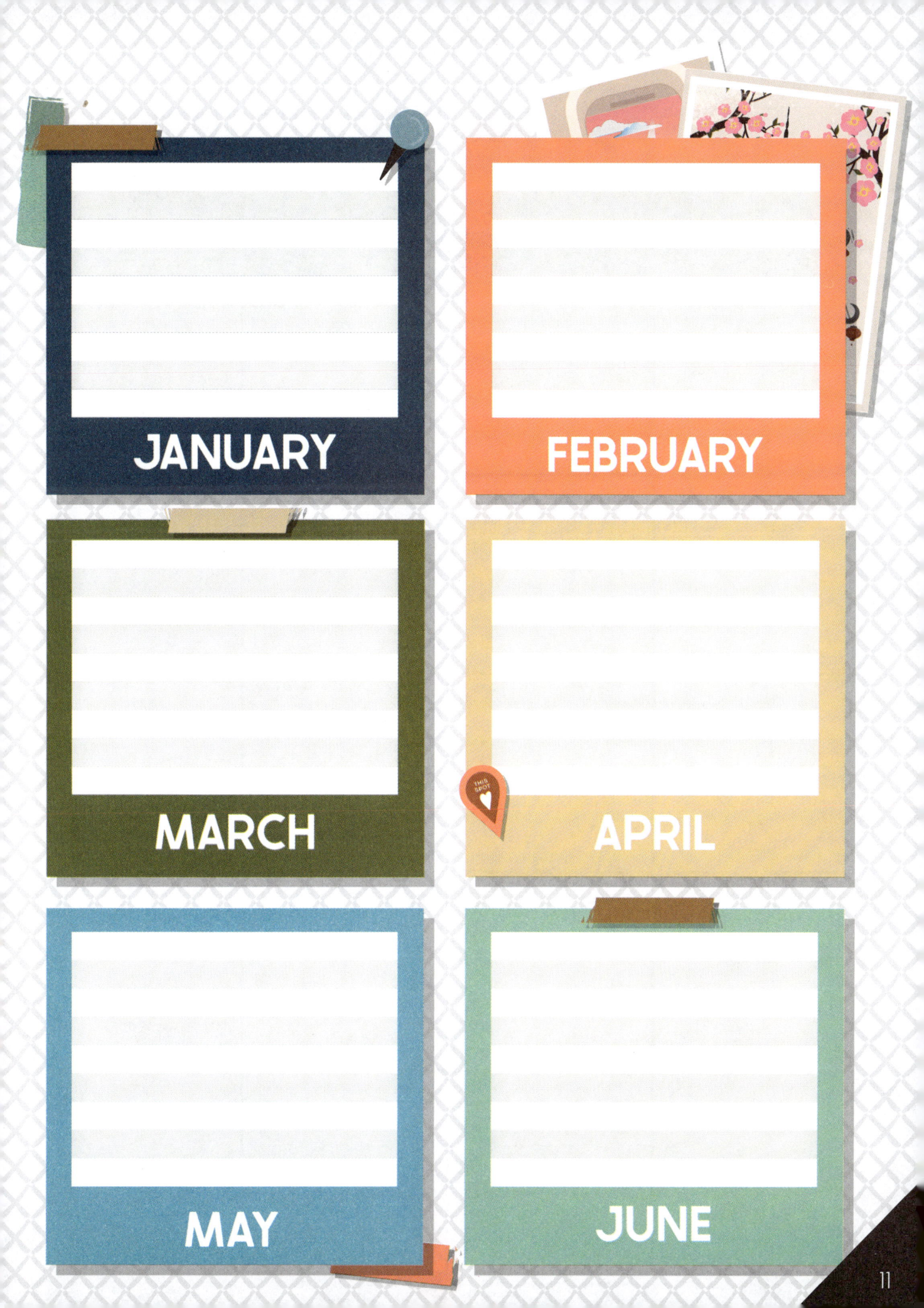

## JANUARY

## FEBRUARY

## MARCH

## APRIL

## MAY

## JUNE

# JULY

*Let curiosity lead the way.*

| SUNDAY | MONDAY | TUESDAY | WEDNESDAY |
|--------|--------|---------|-----------|
|        |        |         |           |
|        |        |         |           |
|        |        |         |           |
|        |        |         |           |
|        |        |         |           |

## IMPORTANT DATES

## GOALS

| THURSDAY | FRIDAY | SATURDAY |
|---|---|---|
|  |  |  |
|  |  |  |
|  |  |  |
|  |  |  |
|  |  |  |

### HAVE TO DO

### NOTES

PSST! USE THESE GUIDES TO KEEP YOUR TABS PERFECTLY PLACED.

# AUGUST

*every day is an adventure.*

| SUNDAY | MONDAY | TUESDAY | WEDNESDAY |
| --- | --- | --- | --- |
|  |  |  |  |
|  |  |  |  |
|  |  |  |  |
|  |  |  |  |
|  |  |  |  |

**IMPORTANT DATES**

**GOALS**

| THURSDAY | FRIDAY | SATURDAY |
|---|---|---|
|  |  |  |
|  |  |  |
|  |  |  |
|  |  |  |
|  |  |  |

**HAVE TO DO**
- 
- 
- 
- 
- 
- 
- 
- 
- 
- 
- 

**NOTES**

# SEPTEMBER

*Today is an open road to your dreams.*

| SUNDAY | MONDAY | TUESDAY | WEDNESDAY |
|--------|--------|---------|-----------|
|        |        |         |           |
|        |        |         |           |
|        |        |         |           |
|        |        |         |           |
|        |        |         |           |

**IMPORTANT DATES**

**GOALS**

| THURSDAY | FRIDAY | SATURDAY |
|---|---|---|
| | | |
| | | |
| | | |
| | | |
| | | |

**HAVE TO DO**
- 
- 
- 
- 
- 
- 
- 
- 
- 
- 
- 

**NOTES**

# OCTOBER

*Expand your horizons.*

| SUNDAY | MONDAY | TUESDAY | WEDNESDAY |
|---|---|---|---|
| | | | |
| | | | |
| | | | |
| | | | |
| | | | |

| IMPORTANT DATES | GOALS |

| THURSDAY | FRIDAY | SATURDAY |
|---|---|---|
| | | |
| | | |
| | | |
| | | |
| | | |

**HAVE TO DO**

**NOTES**

19

# NOVEMBER

*Don't just dream — plan!*

| SUNDAY | MONDAY | TUESDAY | WEDNESDAY |
|--------|--------|---------|-----------|
|        |        |         |           |
|        |        |         |           |
|        |        |         |           |
|        |        |         |           |
|        |        |         |           |

IMPORTANT DATES

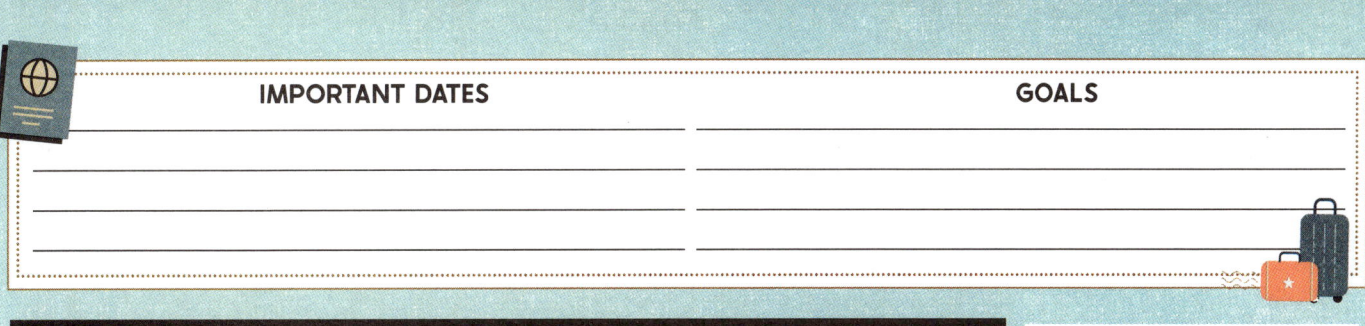

GOALS

| THURSDAY | FRIDAY | SATURDAY |
|---|---|---|
| | | |
| | | |
| | | |
| | | |
| | | |

**HAVE TO DO**

**NOTES**

# DECEMBER

*collect moments, not things.*

| SUNDAY | MONDAY | TUESDAY | WEDNESDAY |
|---|---|---|---|
|  |  |  |  |
|  |  |  |  |
|  |  |  |  |
|  |  |  |  |
|  |  |  |  |

| IMPORTANT DATES | GOALS |
|---|---|

| THURSDAY | FRIDAY | SATURDAY |
|---|---|---|
| | | |
| | | |
| | | |
| | | |
| | | |

**HAVE TO DO**

**NOTES**

# JANUARY

*not all classrooms have four walls.*

| SUNDAY | MONDAY | TUESDAY | WEDNESDAY |
|--------|--------|---------|-----------|
|        |        |         |           |
|        |        |         |           |
|        |        |         |           |
|        |        |         |           |
|        |        |         |           |

| IMPORTANT DATES | GOALS |
|---|---|

| THURSDAY | FRIDAY | SATURDAY |
|---|---|---|

**HAVE TO DO**

**NOTES**

# FEBRUARY

*don't wait for opportunity — create it.*

| SUNDAY | MONDAY | TUESDAY | WEDNESDAY |
|---|---|---|---|
| | | | |
| | | | |
| | | | |
| | | | |
| | | | |

| | IMPORTANT DATES | | GOALS |
|---|---|---|---|

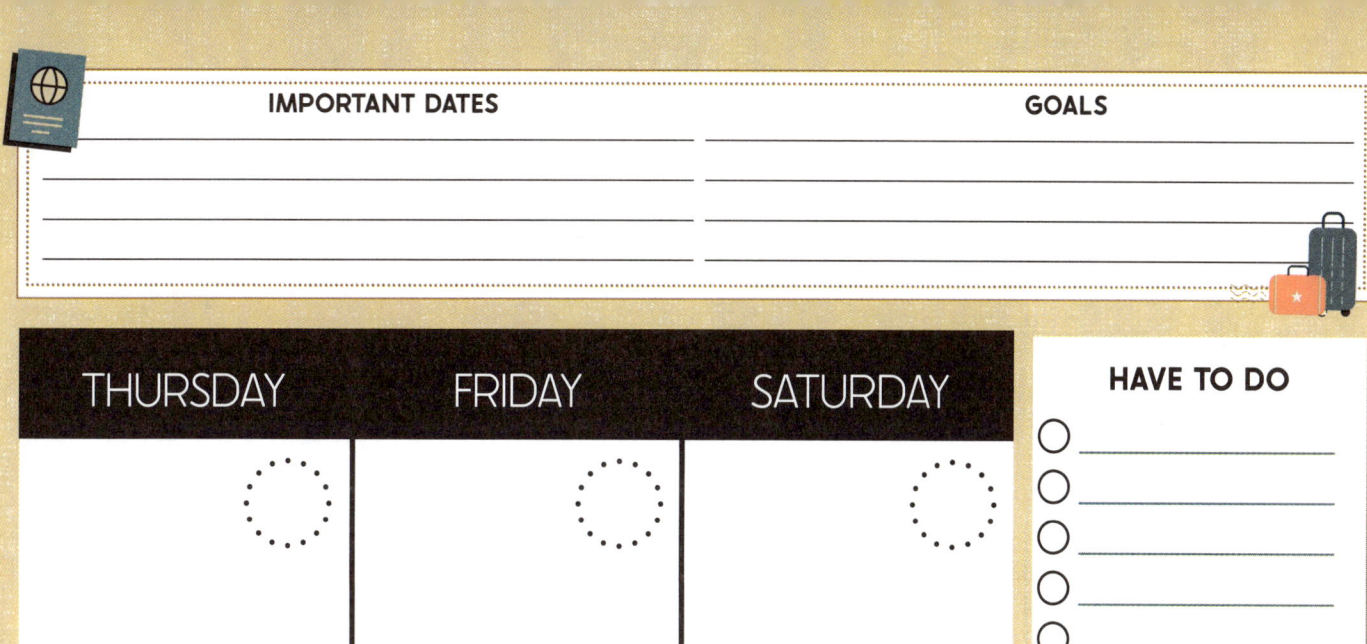

| THURSDAY | FRIDAY | SATURDAY |
|---|---|---|
| | | |
| | | |
| | | |
| | | |
| | | |

**HAVE TO DO**
- ○
- ○
- ○
- ○
- ○
- ○
- ○
- ○
- ○
- ○
- ○
- ○

**NOTES**

# MARCH

*The best view comes after the hardest climb.*

| SUNDAY | MONDAY | TUESDAY | WEDNESDAY |
|--------|--------|---------|-----------|
|        |        |         |           |
|        |        |         |           |
|        |        |         |           |
|        |        |         |           |
|        |        |         |           |

## IMPORTANT DATES

## GOALS

| THURSDAY | FRIDAY | SATURDAY |
|---|---|---|
|  |  |  |
|  |  |  |
|  |  |  |
|  |  |  |
|  |  |  |

## HAVE TO DO

## NOTES

# APRIL

*Every journey needs a first step.*

| SUNDAY | MONDAY | TUESDAY | WEDNESDAY |
|--------|--------|---------|-----------|
|        |        |         |           |
|        |        |         |           |
|        |        |         |           |
|        |        |         |           |
|        |        |         |           |

| IMPORTANT DATES | GOALS |
|---|---|

| THURSDAY | FRIDAY | SATURDAY |
|---|---|---|
|  |  |  |
|  |  |  |
|  |  |  |
|  |  |  |
|  |  |  |

**HAVE TO DO**

**NOTES**

# MAY

GO. DO. LIVE. LOVE.

| SUNDAY | MONDAY | TUESDAY | WEDNESDAY |
|---|---|---|---|
| | | | |
| | | | |
| | | | |
| | | | |
| | | | |

## IMPORTANT DATES

## GOALS

| THURSDAY | FRIDAY | SATURDAY |
|---|---|---|
|  |  |  |
|  |  |  |
|  |  |  |
|  |  |  |
|  |  |  |

### HAVE TO DO

### NOTES

# JUNE

*The world is yours to explore.*

| SUNDAY | MONDAY | TUESDAY | WEDNESDAY |
|--------|--------|---------|-----------|
|        |        |         |           |
|        |        |         |           |
|        |        |         |           |
|        |        |         |           |
|        |        |         |           |

| SUBJECT | SUBJECT | SUBJECT | SUBJECT |
|---------|---------|---------|---------|
|         |         |         |         |

# WEEK #

| | SUBJECT | SUBJECT | SUBJECT |
|---|---|---|---|
| **MONDAY** | Arrival<br>Sign language | | |
| **TUESDAY** | | | |
| **WEDNESDAY** | | | |
| **THURSDAY** | | | |
| **FRIDAY** | | | |

| SUBJECT | SUBJECT | SUBJECT | SUBJECT |
|---------|---------|---------|---------|
|         |         |         |         |
|         |         |         |         |
|         |         |         |         |
|         |         |         |         |
|         |         |         |         |
| SUBJECT | SUBJECT | SUBJECT | SUBJECT |

# WEEK #

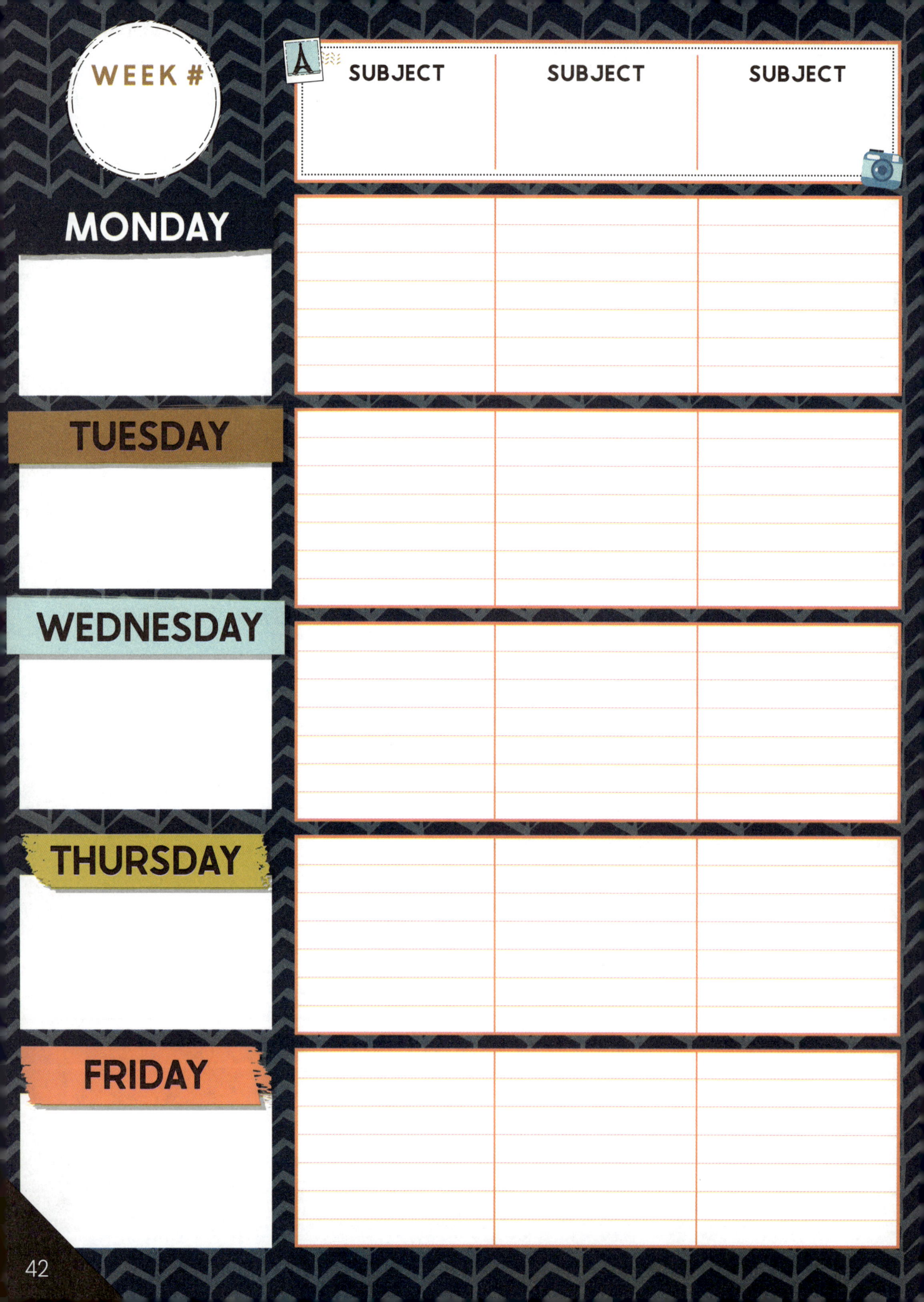

|  | SUBJECT | SUBJECT | SUBJECT |
|---|---|---|---|
| **MONDAY** | | | |
| **TUESDAY** | | | |
| **WEDNESDAY** | | | |
| **THURSDAY** | | | |
| **FRIDAY** | | | |

| SUBJECT | SUBJECT | SUBJECT | SUBJECT |
| --- | --- | --- | --- |
|  |  |  |  |
|  |  |  |  |
|  |  |  |  |
|  |  |  |  |
| SUBJECT | SUBJECT | SUBJECT | SUBJECT |

WEEK #

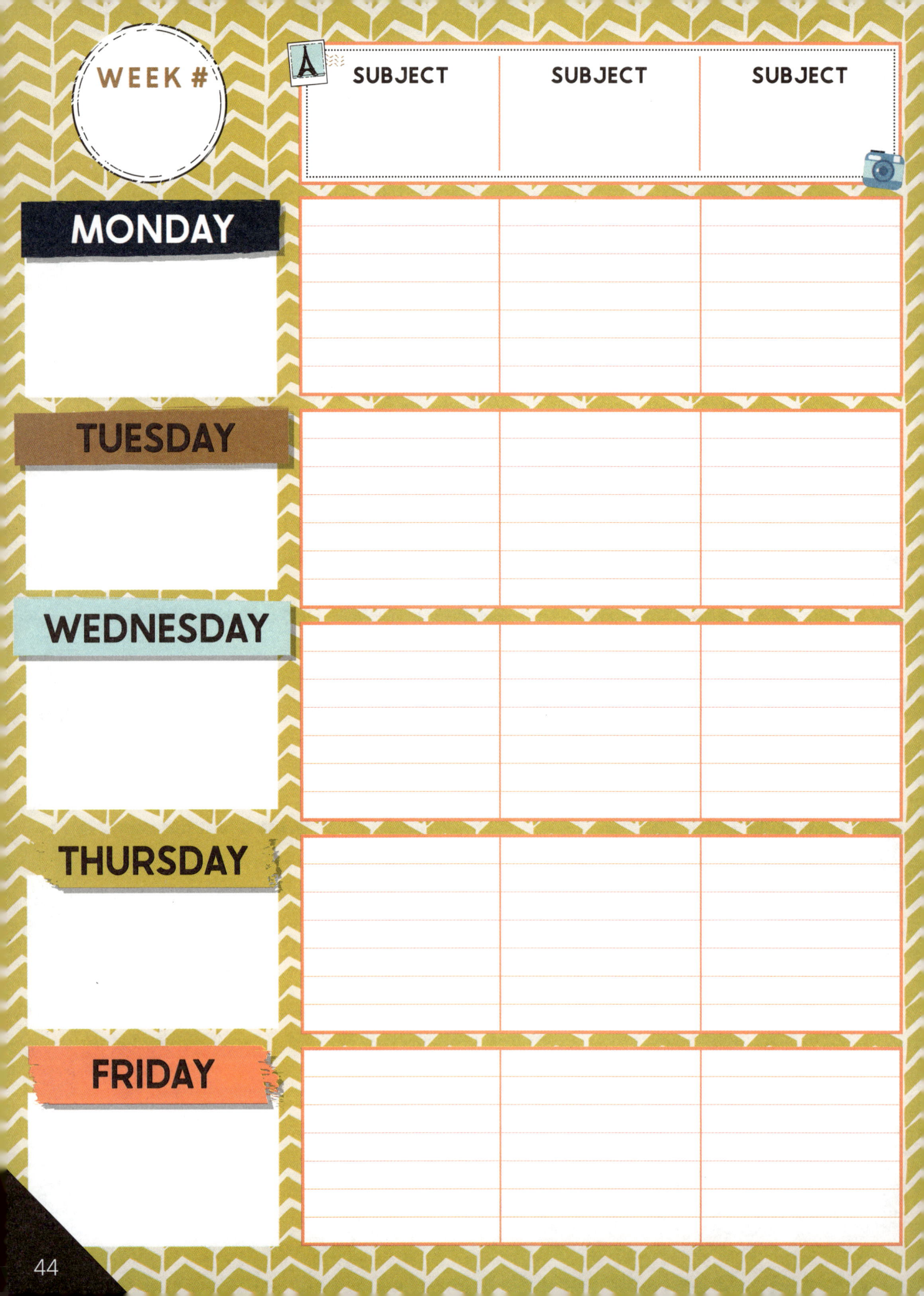

| | SUBJECT | SUBJECT | SUBJECT |
|---|---|---|---|

**MONDAY**

**TUESDAY**

**WEDNESDAY**

**THURSDAY**

**FRIDAY**

44

| SUBJECT | SUBJECT | SUBJECT | SUBJECT |
|---------|---------|---------|---------|
|         |         |         |         |
|         |         |         |         |
|         |         |         |         |
|         |         |         |         |
|         |         |         |         |
| SUBJECT | SUBJECT | SUBJECT | SUBJECT |

WEEK #

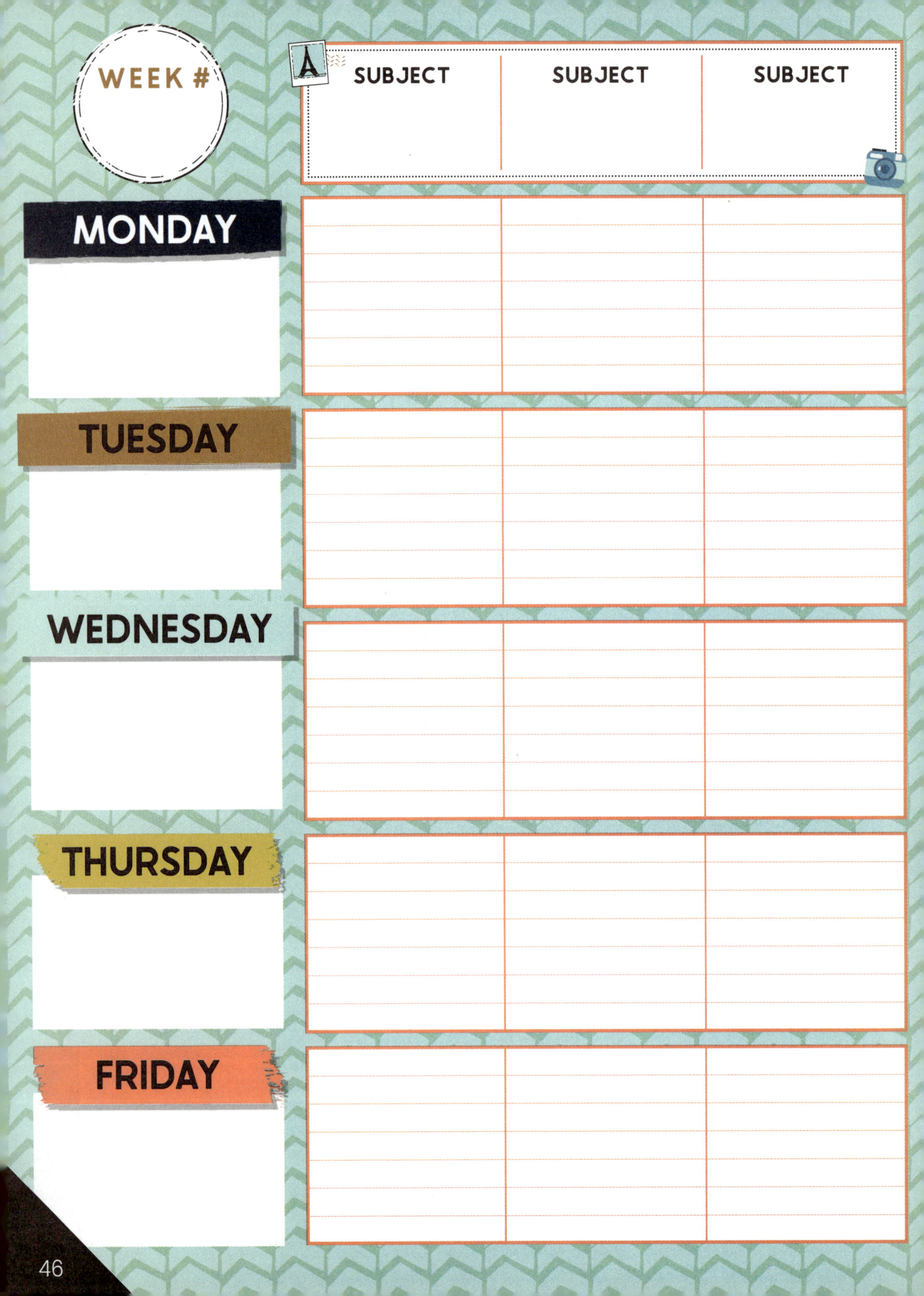

| | SUBJECT | SUBJECT | SUBJECT |
|---|---|---|---|
| **MONDAY** | | | |
| **TUESDAY** | | | |
| **WEDNESDAY** | | | |
| **THURSDAY** | | | |
| **FRIDAY** | | | |

| SUBJECT | SUBJECT | SUBJECT | SUBJECT |
|---|---|---|---|
|  |  |  |  |
|  |  |  |  |
|  |  |  |  |
|  |  |  |  |
| SUBJECT | SUBJECT | SUBJECT | SUBJECT |

WEEK #

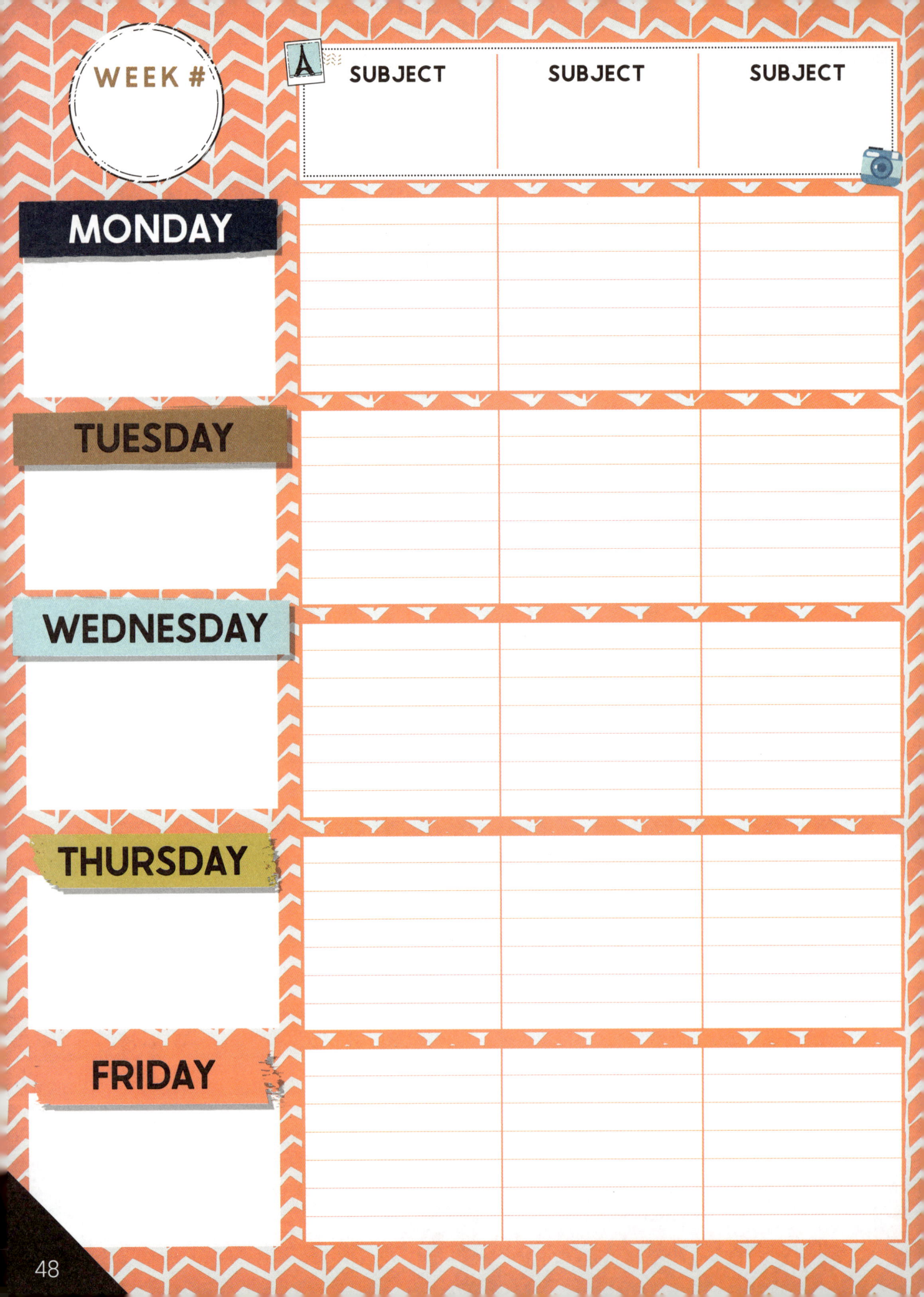

| | SUBJECT | SUBJECT | SUBJECT |
|---|---|---|---|

**MONDAY**

**TUESDAY**

**WEDNESDAY**

**THURSDAY**

**FRIDAY**

| SUBJECT | SUBJECT | SUBJECT | SUBJECT |
|---------|---------|---------|---------|
|         |         |         |         |
|         |         |         |         |
|         |         |         |         |
|         |         |         |         |
|         |         |         |         |

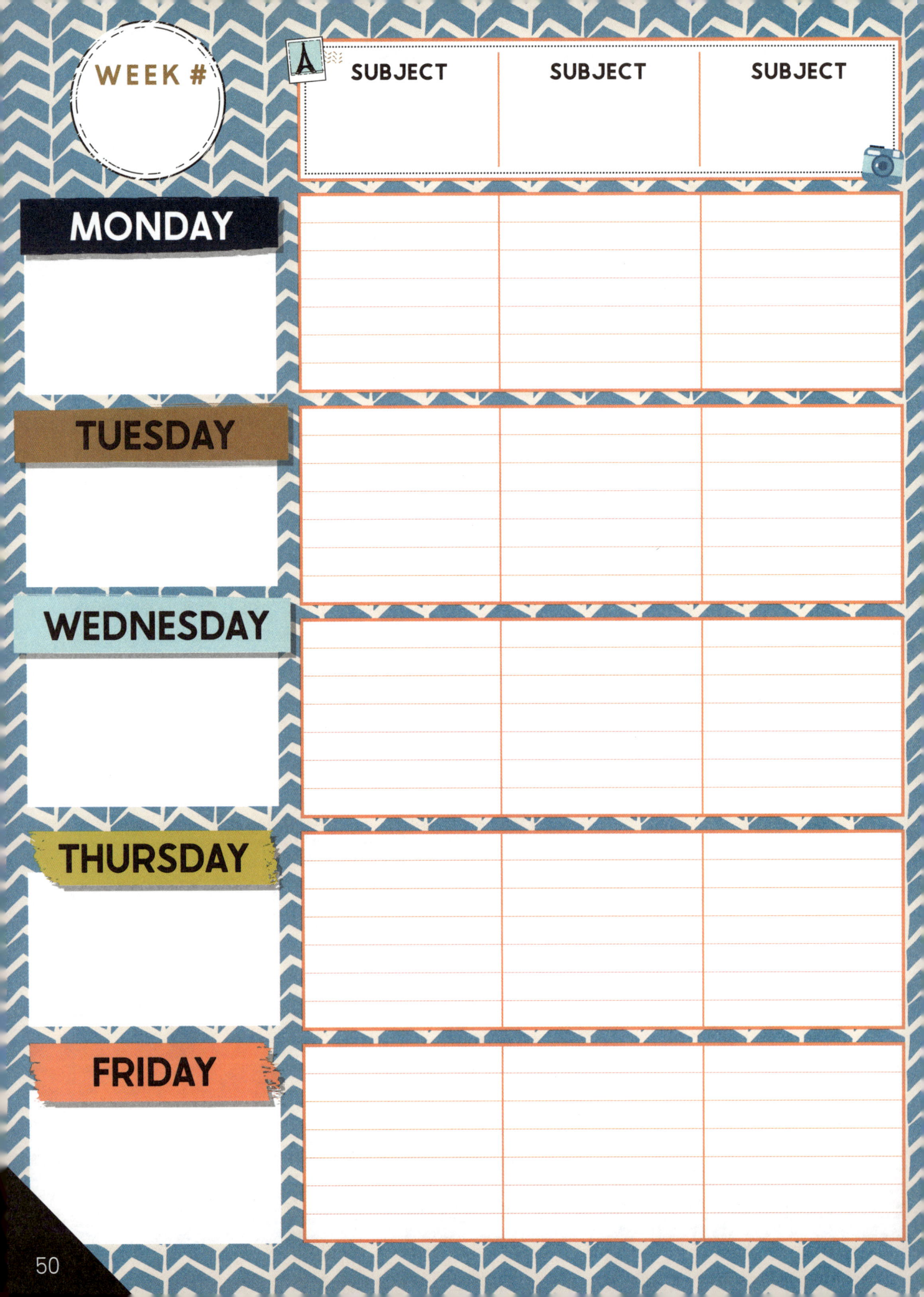

## WEEK #

|  | SUBJECT | SUBJECT | SUBJECT |
|---|---|---|---|
| **MONDAY** | | | |
| **TUESDAY** | | | |
| **WEDNESDAY** | | | |
| **THURSDAY** | | | |
| **FRIDAY** | | | |

| SUBJECT | SUBJECT | SUBJECT | SUBJECT |
|---------|---------|---------|---------|
|         |         |         |         |
|         |         |         |         |
|         |         |         |         |
|         |         |         |         |
|         |         |         |         |

| SUBJECT | SUBJECT | SUBJECT | SUBJECT |
|---------|---------|---------|---------|

# WEEK #

| SUBJECT | SUBJECT | SUBJECT |
|---------|---------|---------|

**MONDAY**

**TUESDAY**

**WEDNESDAY**

**THURSDAY**

**FRIDAY**

| SUBJECT | SUBJECT | SUBJECT |
|---------|---------|---------|

| SUBJECT | SUBJECT | SUBJECT | SUBJECT |
| --- | --- | --- | --- |
|  |  |  |  |
|  |  |  |  |
|  |  |  |  |
|  |  |  |  |
|  |  |  |  |

## WEEK #

|  | SUBJECT | SUBJECT | SUBJECT |
|---|---|---|---|
| **MONDAY** | | | |
| **TUESDAY** | | | |
| **WEDNESDAY** | | | |
| **THURSDAY** | | | |
| **FRIDAY** | | | |

| SUBJECT | SUBJECT | SUBJECT | SUBJECT |
| --- | --- | --- | --- |
| | | | |
| | | | |
| | | | |
| | | | |
| | | | |
| SUBJECT | SUBJECT | SUBJECT | SUBJECT |

# WEEK #

| | SUBJECT | SUBJECT | SUBJECT |
|---|---|---|---|
| **MONDAY** | | | |
| **TUESDAY** | | | |
| **WEDNESDAY** | | | |
| **THURSDAY** | | | |
| **FRIDAY** | | | |
| | SUBJECT | SUBJECT | SUBJECT |

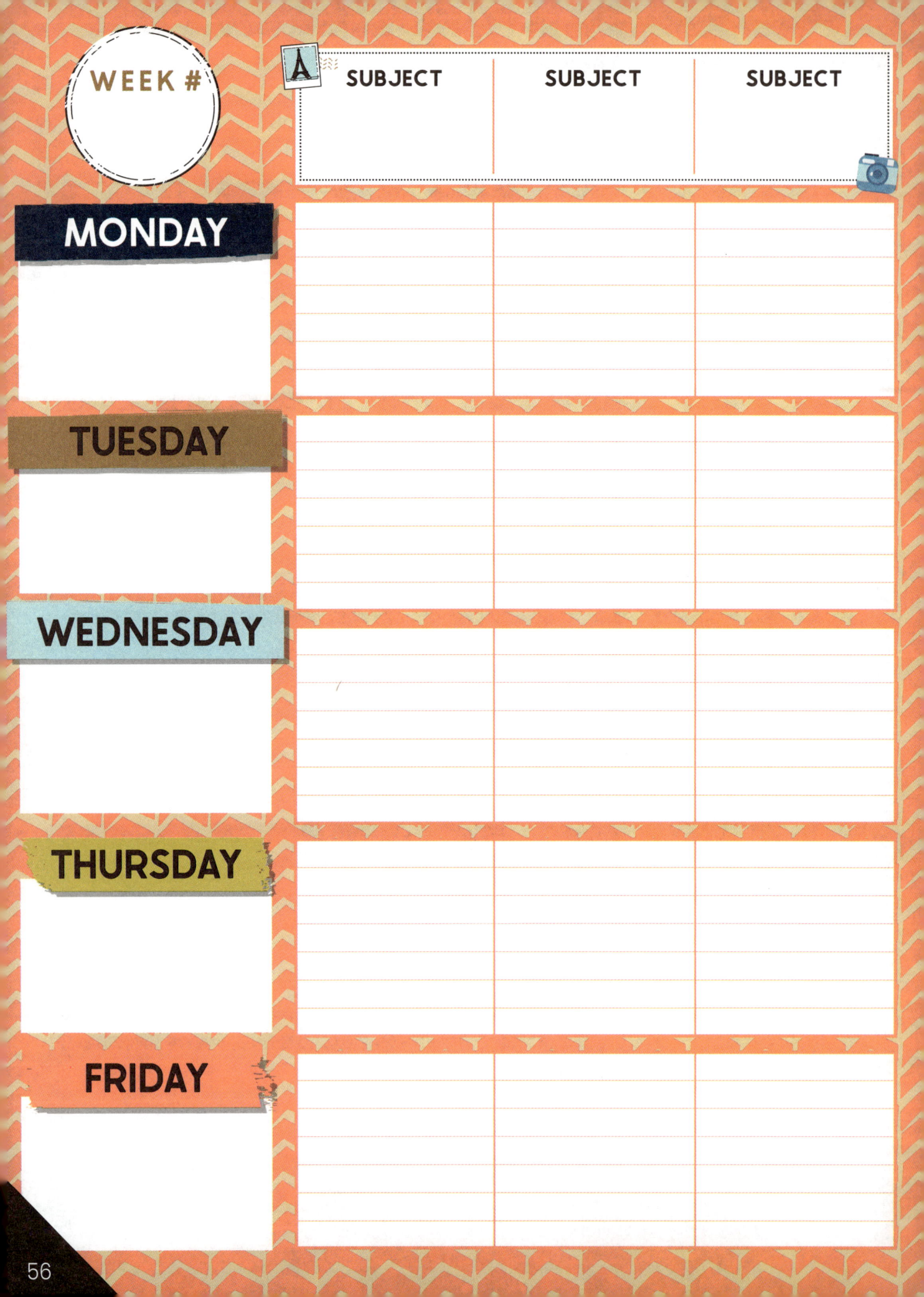

| SUBJECT | SUBJECT | SUBJECT | SUBJECT |
|---------|---------|---------|---------|
|         |         |         |         |
|         |         |         |         |
|         |         |         |         |
|         |         |         |         |
|         |         |         |         |

| SUBJECT | SUBJECT | SUBJECT | SUBJECT |
|---------|---------|---------|---------|

# WEEK #

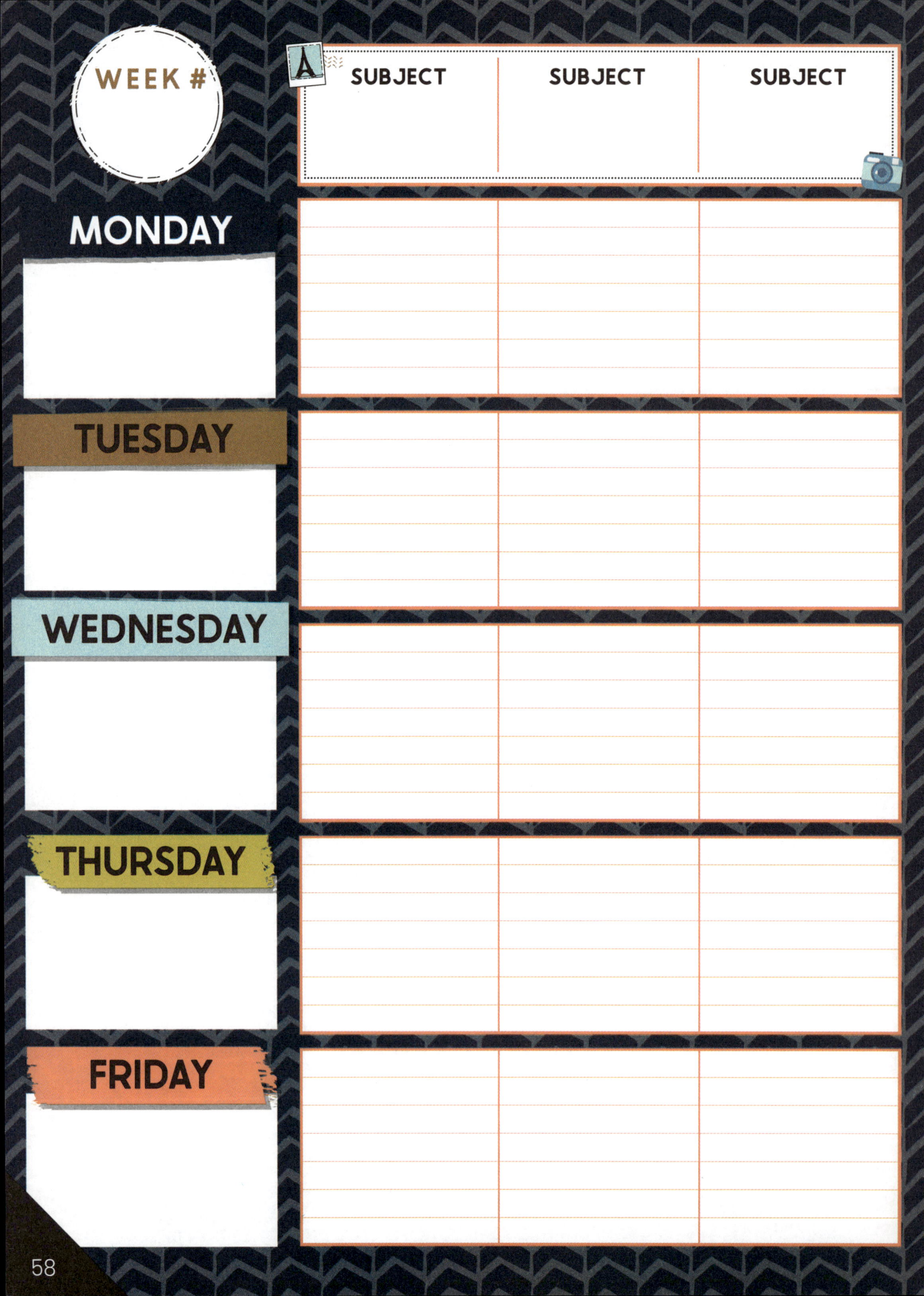

| | SUBJECT | SUBJECT | SUBJECT |
|---|---|---|---|
| **MONDAY** | | | |
| **TUESDAY** | | | |
| **WEDNESDAY** | | | |
| **THURSDAY** | | | |
| **FRIDAY** | | | |

| SUBJECT | SUBJECT | SUBJECT | SUBJECT |
|---------|---------|---------|---------|
|         |         |         |         |
|         |         |         |         |
|         |         |         |         |
|         |         |         |         |
|         |         |         |         |

| SUBJECT | SUBJECT | SUBJECT | SUBJECT |

# WEEK #

| | SUBJECT | SUBJECT | SUBJECT |
|---|---|---|---|

**MONDAY**

**TUESDAY**

**WEDNESDAY**

**THURSDAY**

**FRIDAY**

| SUBJECT | SUBJECT | SUBJECT | SUBJECT |
|---|---|---|---|
| | | | |
| | | | |
| | | | |
| | | | |
| | | | |

| SUBJECT | SUBJECT | SUBJECT | SUBJECT |
|---|---|---|---|

# WEEK #

| SUBJECT | SUBJECT | SUBJECT |
|---------|---------|---------|

**MONDAY**

**TUESDAY**

**WEDNESDAY**

**THURSDAY**

**FRIDAY**

| SUBJECT | SUBJECT | SUBJECT | SUBJECT |
|---------|---------|---------|---------|
|         |         |         |         |
|         |         |         |         |
|         |         |         |         |
|         |         |         |         |
|         |         |         |         |

| SUBJECT | SUBJECT | SUBJECT | SUBJECT |
|---------|---------|---------|---------|

# WEEK #

| | SUBJECT | SUBJECT | SUBJECT |
|---|---|---|---|

**MONDAY**

**TUESDAY**

**WEDNESDAY**

**THURSDAY**

**FRIDAY**

| | SUBJECT | SUBJECT | SUBJECT |
|---|---|---|---|

| SUBJECT | SUBJECT | SUBJECT | SUBJECT |
|---------|---------|---------|---------|
|         |         |         |         |
|         |         |         |         |
|         |         |         |         |
|         |         |         |         |
|         |         |         |         |
| SUBJECT | SUBJECT | SUBJECT | SUBJECT |

# WEEK #

|  | SUBJECT | SUBJECT | SUBJECT |
|---|---|---|---|
| **MONDAY** | | | |
| **TUESDAY** | | | |
| **WEDNESDAY** | | | |
| **THURSDAY** | | | |
| **FRIDAY** | | | |
|  | SUBJECT | SUBJECT | SUBJECT |

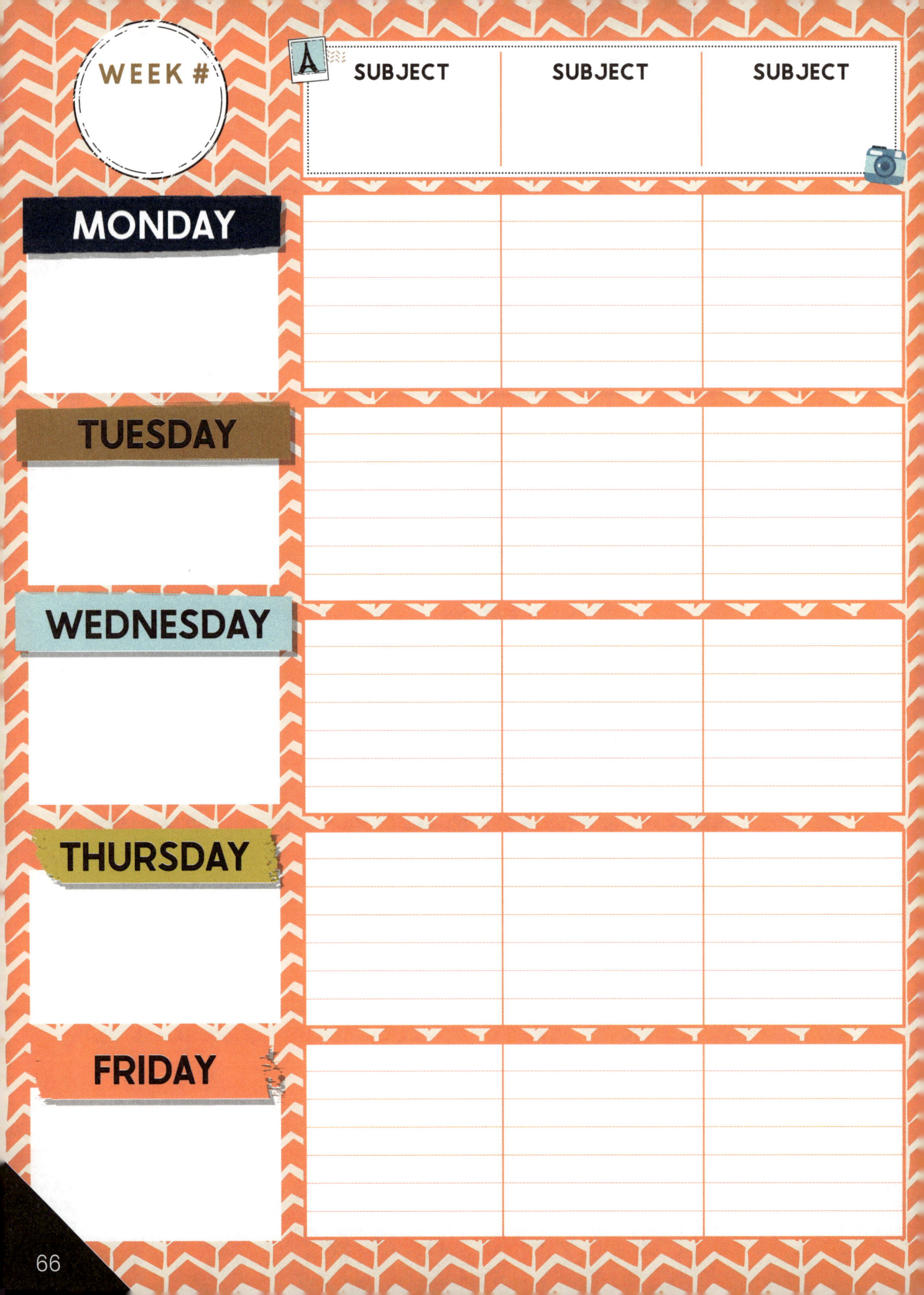

| SUBJECT | SUBJECT | SUBJECT | SUBJECT |
|---------|---------|---------|---------|
|         |         |         |         |
|         |         |         |         |
|         |         |         |         |
|         |         |         |         |

# WEEK #

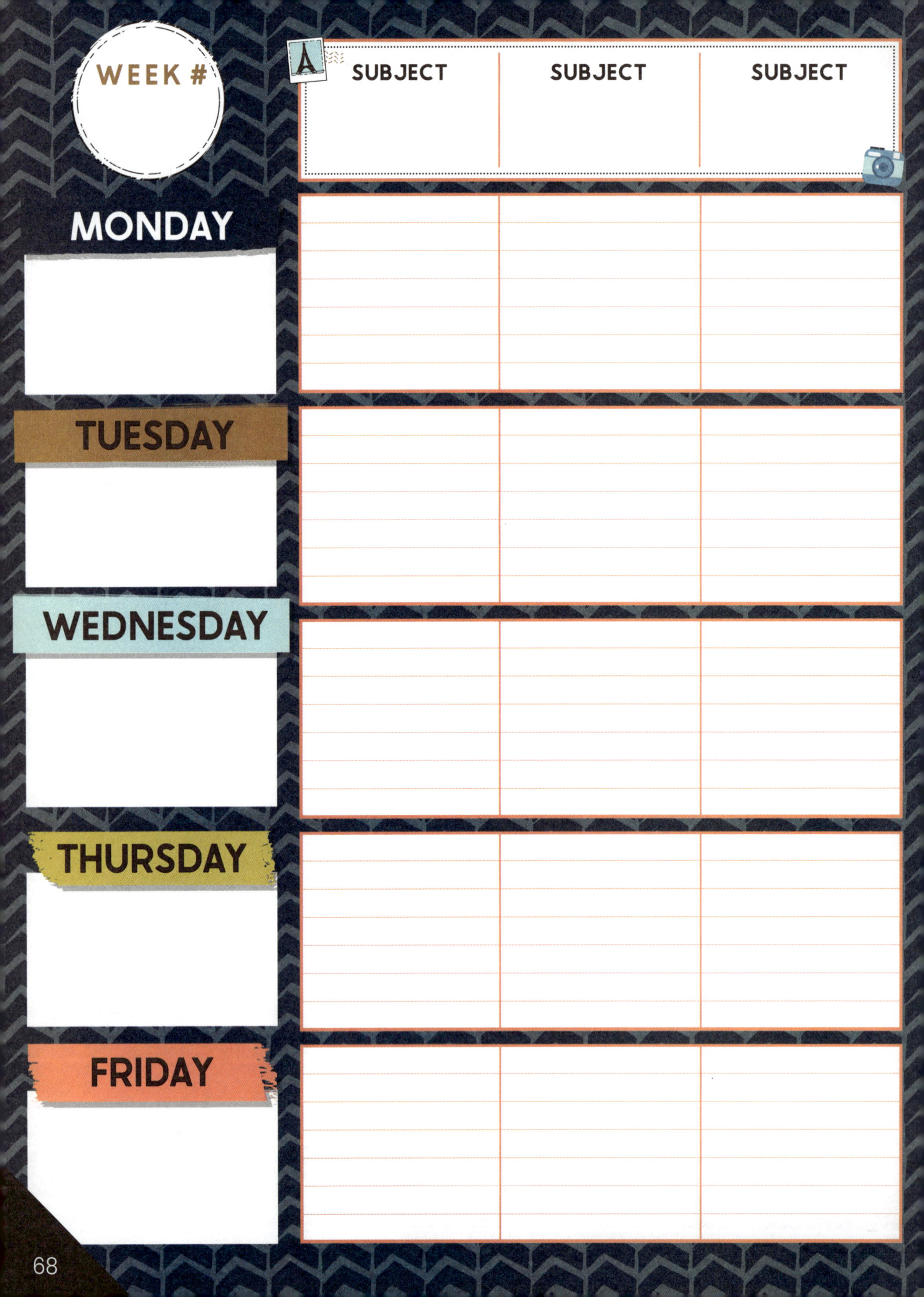

| | SUBJECT | SUBJECT | SUBJECT |
|---|---|---|---|
| **MONDAY** | | | |
| **TUESDAY** | | | |
| **WEDNESDAY** | | | |
| **THURSDAY** | | | |
| **FRIDAY** | | | |

| SUBJECT | SUBJECT | SUBJECT | SUBJECT |
|---------|---------|---------|---------|
|         |         |         |         |
|         |         |         |         |
|         |         |         |         |
|         |         |         |         |
| SUBJECT | SUBJECT | SUBJECT | SUBJECT |

# WEEK #

| SUBJECT | SUBJECT | SUBJECT |
|---------|---------|---------|

**MONDAY**

**TUESDAY**

**WEDNESDAY**

**THURSDAY**

**FRIDAY**

| SUBJECT | SUBJECT | SUBJECT |
|---------|---------|---------|

| SUBJECT | SUBJECT | SUBJECT | SUBJECT |
|---------|---------|---------|---------|
|         |         |         |         |
|         |         |         |         |
|         |         |         |         |
|         |         |         |         |

# WEEK #

| SUBJECT | SUBJECT | SUBJECT |
|---------|---------|---------|

**MONDAY**

**TUESDAY**

**WEDNESDAY**

**THURSDAY**

**FRIDAY**

| SUBJECT | SUBJECT | SUBJECT | SUBJECT |
| --- | --- | --- | --- |
|  |  |  |  |
|  |  |  |  |
|  |  |  |  |
|  |  |  |  |
|  |  |  |  |

# WEEK #

| SUBJECT | SUBJECT | SUBJECT |
|---|---|---|

**MONDAY**

**TUESDAY**

**WEDNESDAY**

**THURSDAY**

**FRIDAY**

| SUBJECT | SUBJECT | SUBJECT | SUBJECT |
|---------|---------|---------|---------|
|         |         |         |         |
|         |         |         |         |
|         |         |         |         |
|         |         |         |         |
| SUBJECT | SUBJECT | SUBJECT | SUBJECT |

WEEK #

| | SUBJECT | SUBJECT | SUBJECT |
|---|---|---|---|
| **MONDAY** | | | |
| **TUESDAY** | | | |
| **WEDNESDAY** | | | |
| **THURSDAY** | | | |
| **FRIDAY** | | | |
| | SUBJECT | SUBJECT | SUBJECT |

| SUBJECT | SUBJECT | SUBJECT | SUBJECT |
|---------|---------|---------|---------|
|         |         |         |         |
|         |         |         |         |
|         |         |         |         |
|         |         |         |         |
|         |         |         |         |

| SUBJECT | SUBJECT | SUBJECT | SUBJECT |
|---------|---------|---------|---------|

# WEEK #

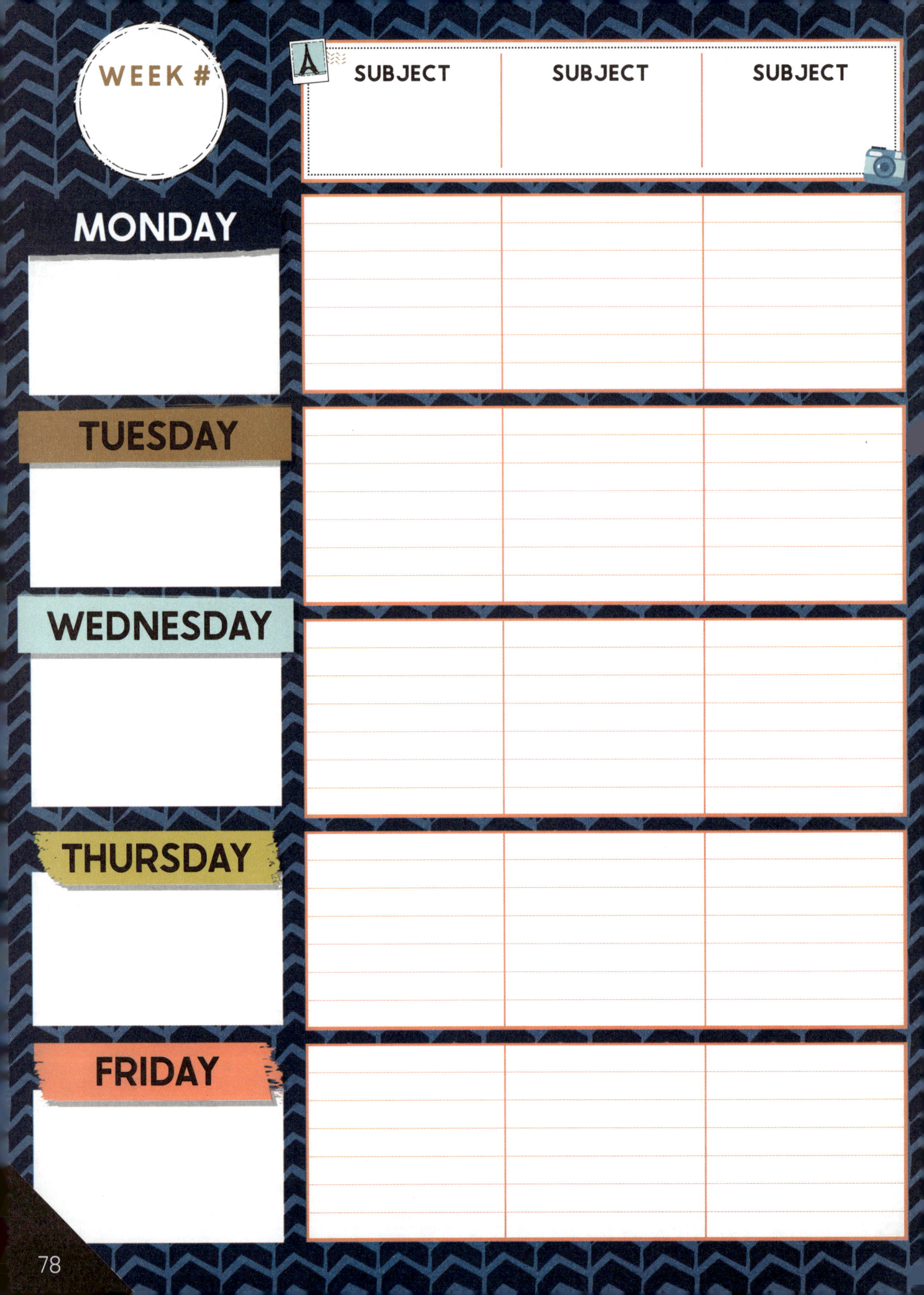

| SUBJECT | SUBJECT | SUBJECT |
|---------|---------|---------|

**MONDAY**

**TUESDAY**

**WEDNESDAY**

**THURSDAY**

**FRIDAY**

| SUBJECT | SUBJECT | SUBJECT | SUBJECT |
|---------|---------|---------|---------|
|         |         |         |         |
|         |         |         |         |
|         |         |         |         |
|         |         |         |         |

# WEEK #

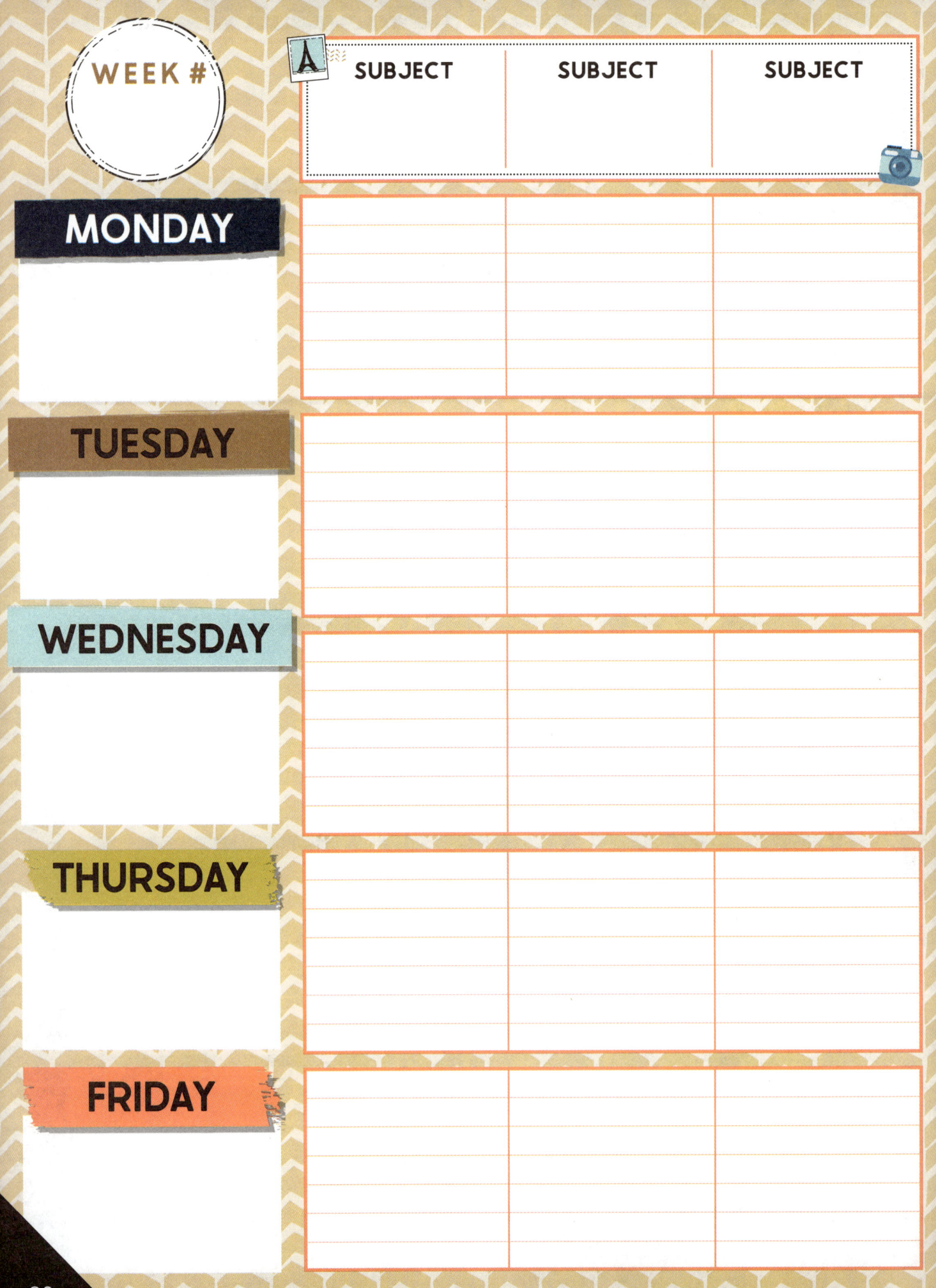

| SUBJECT | SUBJECT | SUBJECT |
|---------|---------|---------|

**MONDAY**

**TUESDAY**

**WEDNESDAY**

**THURSDAY**

**FRIDAY**

| SUBJECT | SUBJECT | SUBJECT | SUBJECT |
|---------|---------|---------|---------|
|         |         |         |         |
|         |         |         |         |
|         |         |         |         |
|         |         |         |         |
|         |         |         |         |

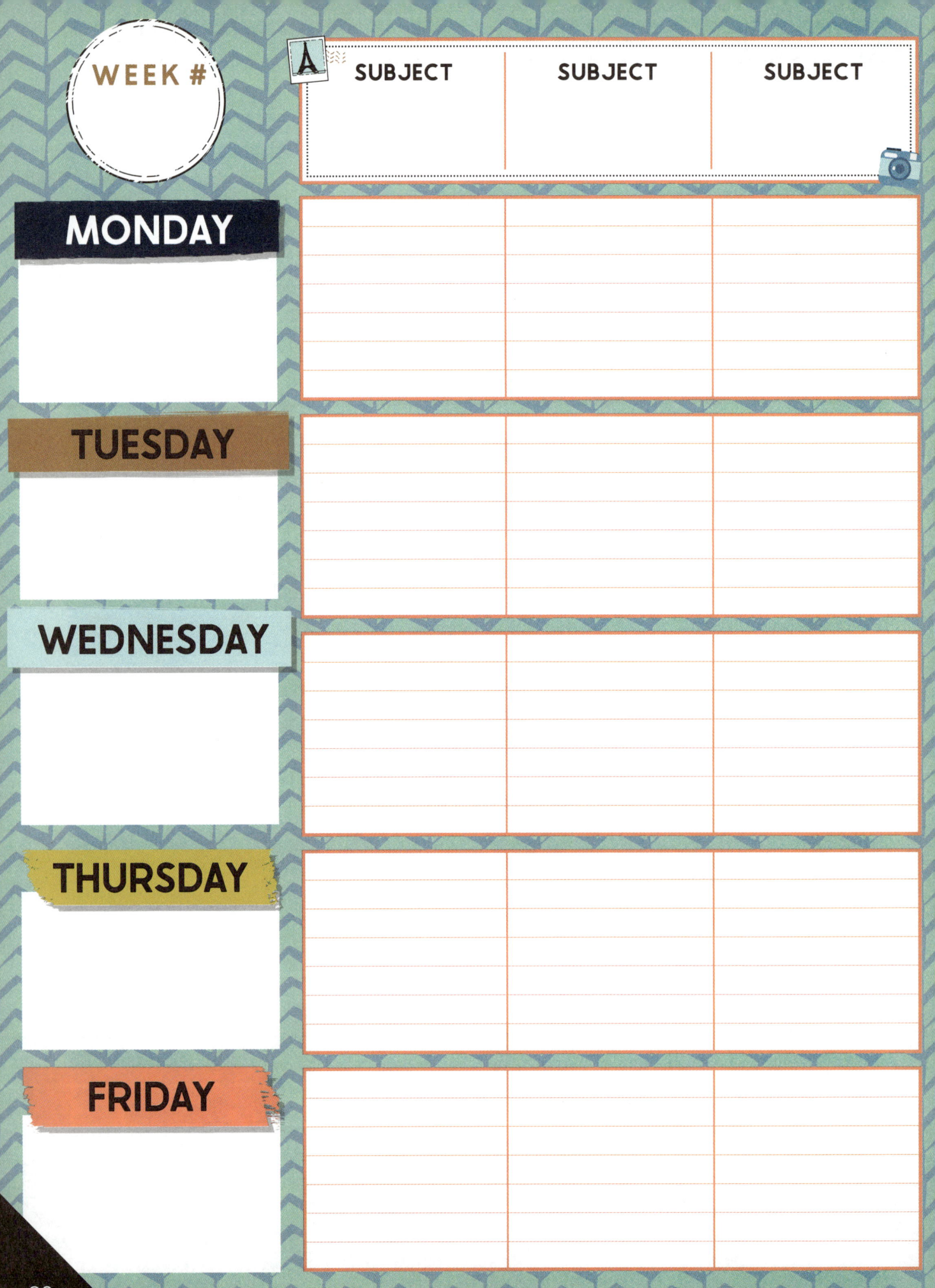

# WEEK #

| SUBJECT | SUBJECT | SUBJECT |
|---------|---------|---------|
| **MONDAY** | | |
| **TUESDAY** | | |
| **WEDNESDAY** | | |
| **THURSDAY** | | |
| **FRIDAY** | | |

| SUBJECT | SUBJECT | SUBJECT | SUBJECT |
| --- | --- | --- | --- |
|  |  |  |  |
|  |  |  |  |
|  |  |  |  |
|  |  |  |  |
|  |  |  |  |
|  |  |  |  |
|  |  |  |  |
|  |  |  |  |
|  |  |  |  |
|  |  |  |  |

| SUBJECT | SUBJECT | SUBJECT | SUBJECT |

# WEEK #

| SUBJECT | SUBJECT | SUBJECT |
|---------|---------|---------|

**MONDAY**

**TUESDAY**

**WEDNESDAY**

**THURSDAY**

**FRIDAY**

| SUBJECT | SUBJECT | SUBJECT | SUBJECT |
|---------|---------|---------|---------|
|         |         |         |         |
|         |         |         |         |
|         |         |         |         |
| SUBJECT | SUBJECT | SUBJECT | SUBJECT |

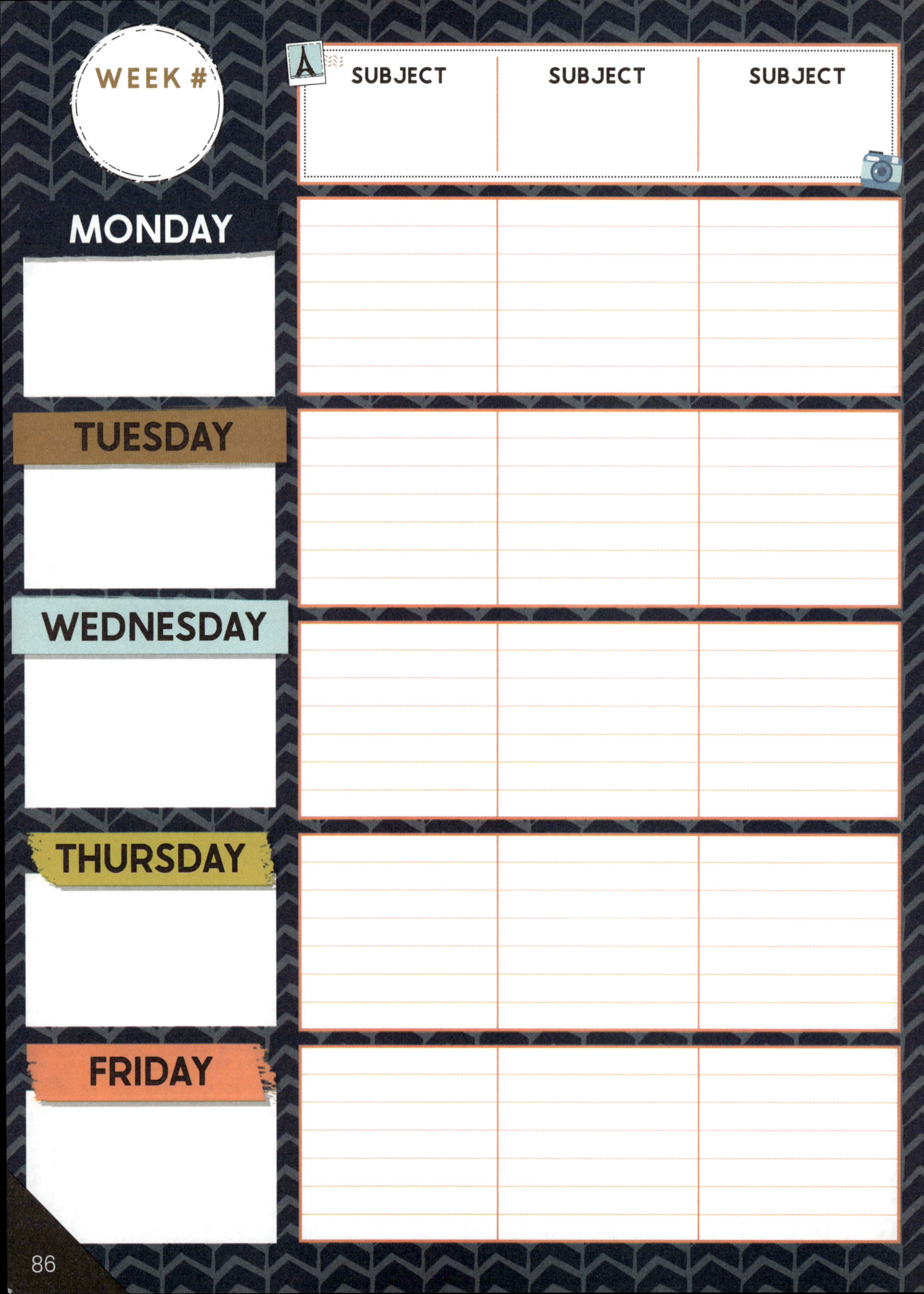

# WEEK #

|  | SUBJECT | SUBJECT | SUBJECT |
|---|---|---|---|
| **MONDAY** | | | |
| **TUESDAY** | | | |
| **WEDNESDAY** | | | |
| **THURSDAY** | | | |
| **FRIDAY** | | | |

| SUBJECT | SUBJECT | SUBJECT | SUBJECT |
|---------|---------|---------|---------|
|         |         |         |         |
|         |         |         |         |
|         |         |         |         |
|         |         |         |         |
|         |         |         |         |
| SUBJECT | SUBJECT | SUBJECT | SUBJECT |

# WEEK #

|  | SUBJECT | SUBJECT | SUBJECT |
|---|---|---|---|
| **MONDAY** | | | |
| **TUESDAY** | | | |
| **WEDNESDAY** | | | |
| **THURSDAY** | | | |
| **FRIDAY** | | | |

| SUBJECT | SUBJECT | SUBJECT | SUBJECT |
|---------|---------|---------|---------|
|         |         |         |         |
|         |         |         |         |
|         |         |         |         |
|         |         |         |         |
|         |         |         |         |

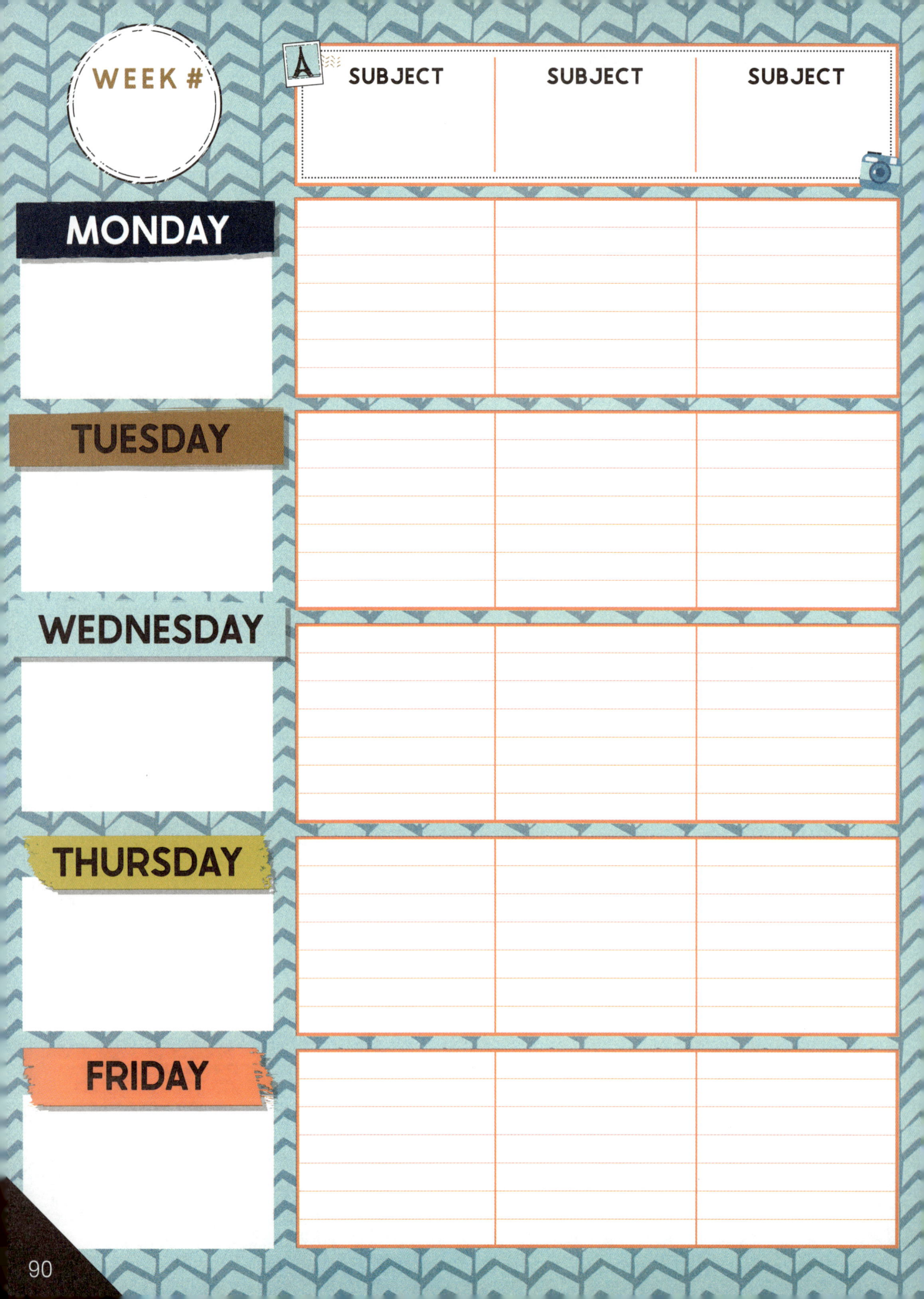

# WEEK #

| | SUBJECT | SUBJECT | SUBJECT |
|---|---|---|---|
| **MONDAY** | | | |
| **TUESDAY** | | | |
| **WEDNESDAY** | | | |
| **THURSDAY** | | | |
| **FRIDAY** | | | |

| SUBJECT | SUBJECT | SUBJECT | SUBJECT |
|---------|---------|---------|---------|
|         |         |         |         |
|         |         |         |         |
|         |         |         |         |
|         |         |         |         |
|         |         |         |         |
| SUBJECT | SUBJECT | SUBJECT | SUBJECT |

# WEEK #

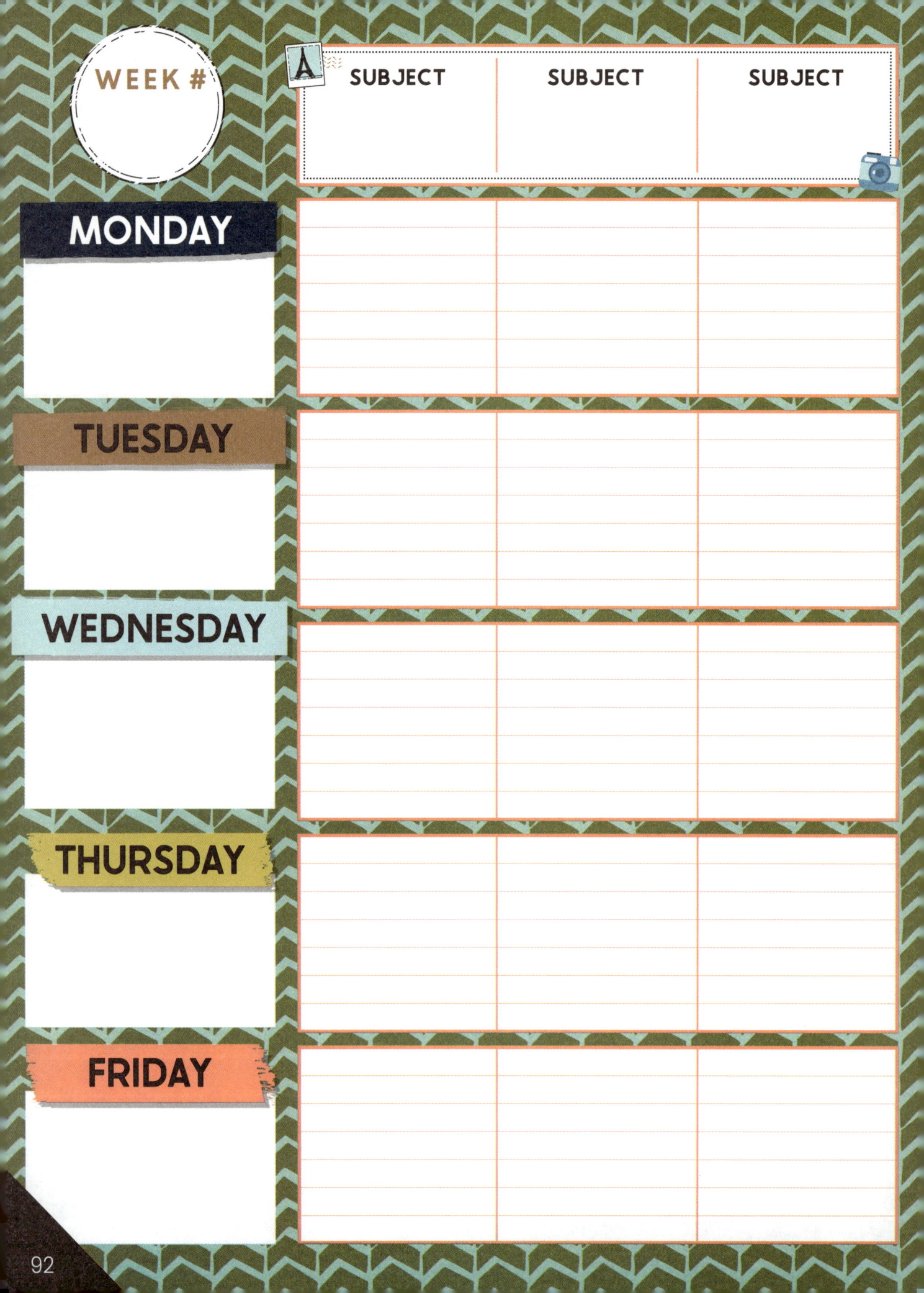

| | SUBJECT | SUBJECT | SUBJECT |
|---|---|---|---|
| **MONDAY** | | | |
| **TUESDAY** | | | |
| **WEDNESDAY** | | | |
| **THURSDAY** | | | |
| **FRIDAY** | | | |
| | SUBJECT | SUBJECT | SUBJECT |

| SUBJECT | SUBJECT | SUBJECT | SUBJECT |
| --- | --- | --- | --- |
|  |  |  |  |
|  |  |  |  |
|  |  |  |  |
|  |  |  |  |
|  |  |  |  |
| SUBJECT | SUBJECT | SUBJECT | SUBJECT |

# WEEK #

| SUBJECT | SUBJECT | SUBJECT |
|---------|---------|---------|

**MONDAY**

**TUESDAY**

**WEDNESDAY**

**THURSDAY**

**FRIDAY**

| SUBJECT | SUBJECT | SUBJECT |
|---------|---------|---------|

| SUBJECT | SUBJECT | SUBJECT | SUBJECT |
| --- | --- | --- | --- |
|  |  |  |  |
|  |  |  |  |
|  |  |  |  |
|  |  |  |  |
|  |  |  |  |

| SUBJECT | SUBJECT | SUBJECT | SUBJECT |
| --- | --- | --- | --- |

WEEK #

| SUBJECT | SUBJECT | SUBJECT |
|---------|---------|---------|

**MONDAY**

**TUESDAY**

**WEDNESDAY**

**THURSDAY**

**FRIDAY**

| SUBJECT | SUBJECT | SUBJECT | SUBJECT |
|---------|---------|---------|---------|
|         |         |         |         |
|         |         |         |         |
|         |         |         |         |
|         |         |         |         |
|         |         |         |         |

| SUBJECT | SUBJECT | SUBJECT | SUBJECT |

# WEEK #

| | SUBJECT | SUBJECT | SUBJECT |
|---|---|---|---|
| **MONDAY** | | | |
| **TUESDAY** | | | |
| **WEDNESDAY** | | | |
| **THURSDAY** | | | |
| **FRIDAY** | | | |
| | SUBJECT | SUBJECT | SUBJECT |

| SUBJECT | SUBJECT | SUBJECT | SUBJECT |
|---------|---------|---------|---------|
|         |         |         |         |
|         |         |         |         |
|         |         |         |         |
|         |         |         |         |
| SUBJECT | SUBJECT | SUBJECT | SUBJECT |

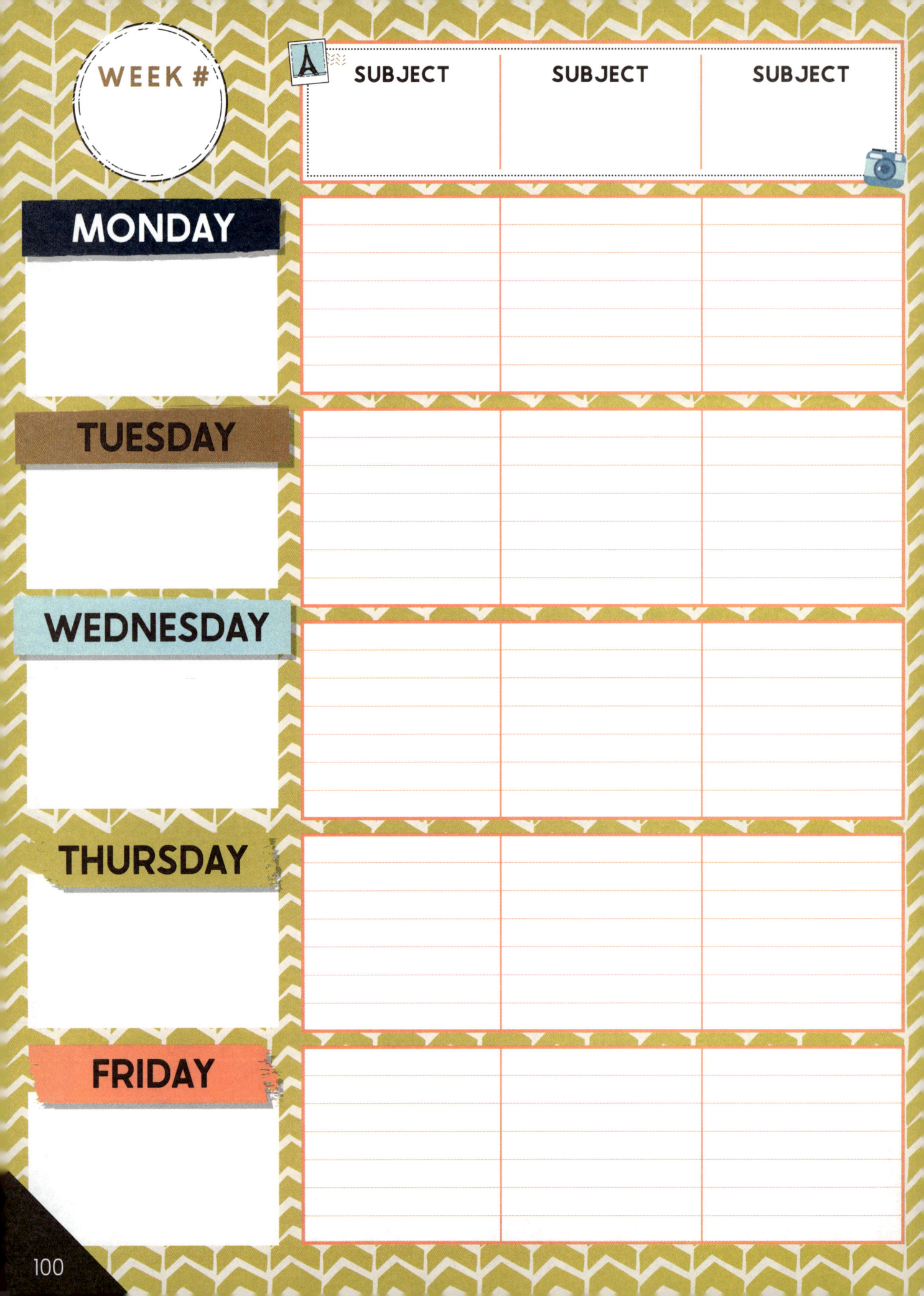

# WEEK #

| SUBJECT | SUBJECT | SUBJECT |
|---------|---------|---------|
| | | |

**MONDAY**

**TUESDAY**

**WEDNESDAY**

**THURSDAY**

**FRIDAY**

| SUBJECT | SUBJECT | SUBJECT |
|---------|---------|---------|

| SUBJECT | SUBJECT | SUBJECT | SUBJECT |
|---------|---------|---------|---------|
|         |         |         |         |
|         |         |         |         |
|         |         |         |         |
|         |         |         |         |
|         |         |         |         |
| SUBJECT | SUBJECT | SUBJECT | SUBJECT |

# WEEK #

| | SUBJECT | SUBJECT | SUBJECT |
|---|---|---|---|
| **MONDAY** | | | |
| **TUESDAY** | | | |
| **WEDNESDAY** | | | |
| **THURSDAY** | | | |
| **FRIDAY** | | | |

| SUBJECT | SUBJECT | SUBJECT | SUBJECT |
|---------|---------|---------|---------|
|         |         |         |         |
|         |         |         |         |
|         |         |         |         |
|         |         |         |         |
| SUBJECT | SUBJECT | SUBJECT | SUBJECT |

# WEEK #

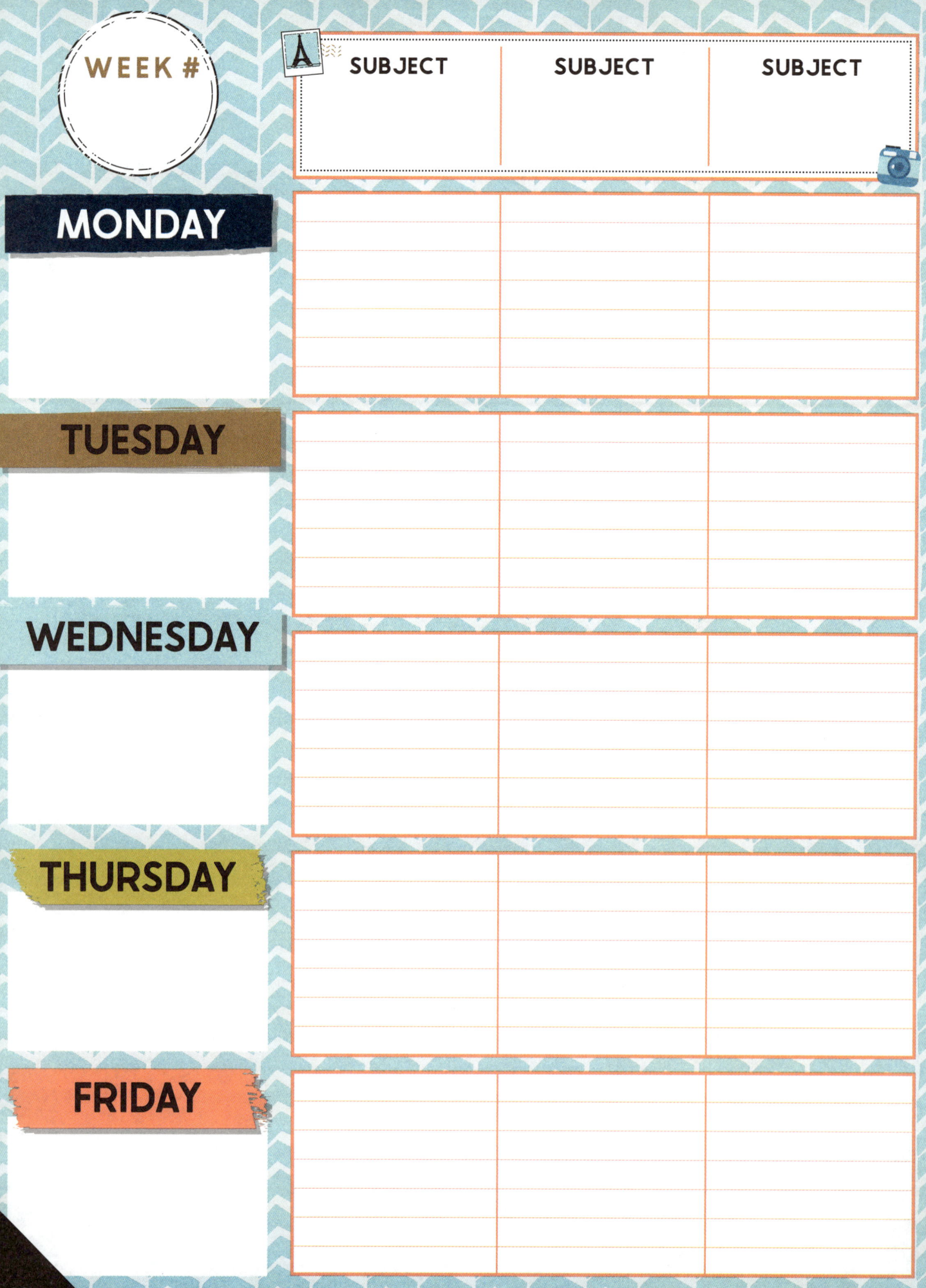

| SUBJECT | SUBJECT | SUBJECT |
|---------|---------|---------|

**MONDAY**

**TUESDAY**

**WEDNESDAY**

**THURSDAY**

**FRIDAY**

| SUBJECT | SUBJECT | SUBJECT | SUBJECT |
| --- | --- | --- | --- |
|  |  |  |  |
|  |  |  |  |
|  |  |  |  |
|  |  |  |  |
|  |  |  |  |
| SUBJECT | SUBJECT | SUBJECT | SUBJECT |

# WEEK #

| | SUBJECT | SUBJECT | SUBJECT |
|---|---|---|---|
| **MONDAY** | | | |
| **TUESDAY** | | | |
| **WEDNESDAY** | | | |
| **THURSDAY** | | | |
| **FRIDAY** | | | |

| SUBJECT | SUBJECT | SUBJECT | SUBJECT |
| --- | --- | --- | --- |
|  |  |  |  |
|  |  |  |  |
|  |  |  |  |
|  |  |  |  |
|  |  |  |  |

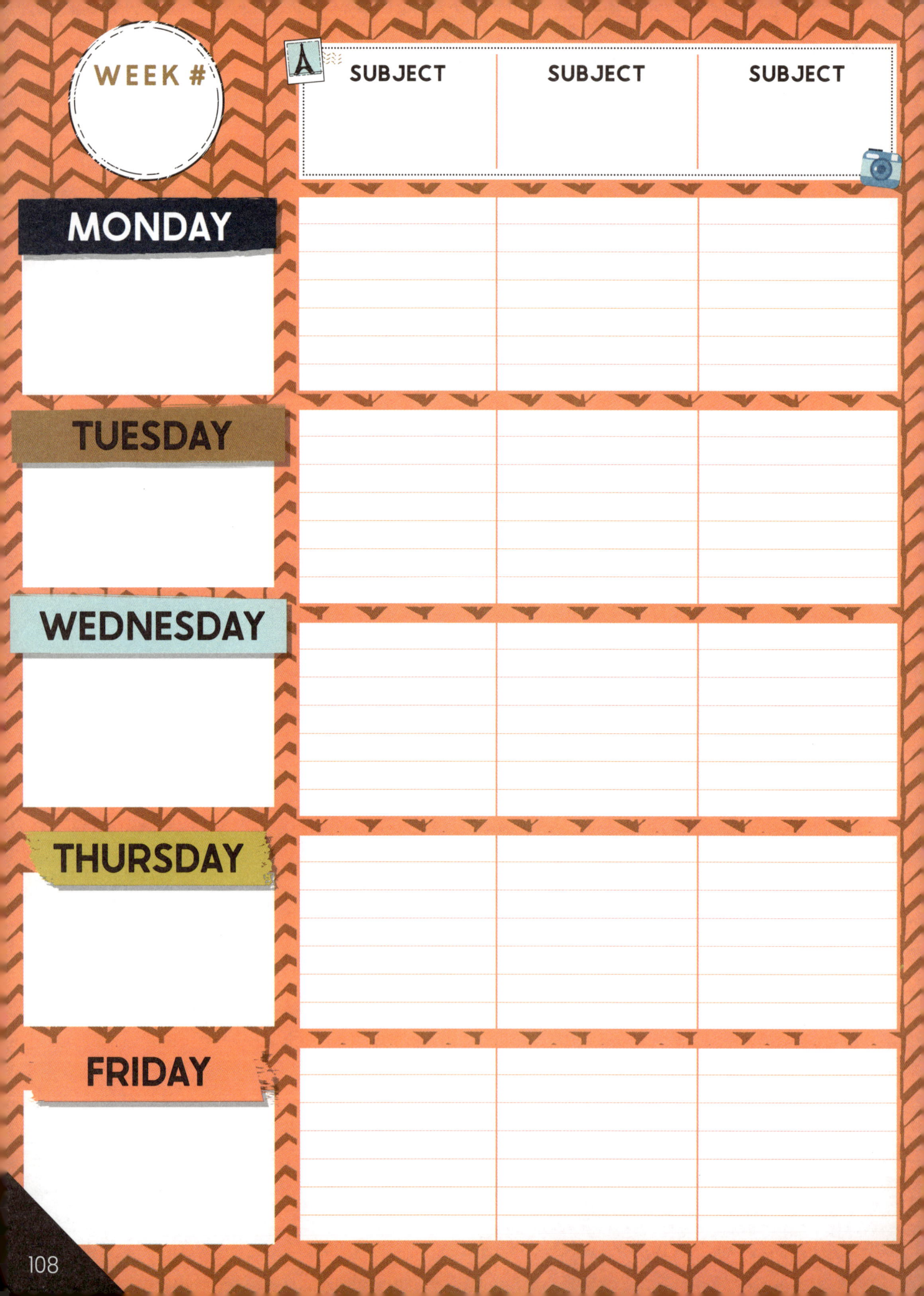

# WEEK #

| SUBJECT | SUBJECT | SUBJECT |
|---------|---------|---------|

**MONDAY**

**TUESDAY**

**WEDNESDAY**

**THURSDAY**

**FRIDAY**

| SUBJECT | SUBJECT | SUBJECT | SUBJECT |
|---------|---------|---------|---------|
|         |         |         |         |
|         |         |         |         |
|         |         |         |         |
|         |         |         |         |
|         |         |         |         |
| SUBJECT | SUBJECT | SUBJECT | SUBJECT |

# WEEK #

|  | SUBJECT | SUBJECT | SUBJECT |
|---|---|---|---|
| **MONDAY** | | | |
| **TUESDAY** | | | |
| **WEDNESDAY** | | | |
| **THURSDAY** | | | |
| **FRIDAY** | | | |
|  | SUBJECT | SUBJECT | SUBJECT |

|         |         |         |         |
|---------|---------|---------|---------|
| SUBJECT | SUBJECT | SUBJECT | SUBJECT |

|  |  |  |  |
|--|--|--|--|
|  |  |  |  |
|  |  |  |  |
|  |  |  |  |
|  |  |  |  |

|  |  |  |  |
|--|--|--|--|
|  |  |  |  |
|  |  |  |  |
|  |  |  |  |
|  |  |  |  |

|  |  |  |  |
|--|--|--|--|
|  |  |  |  |
|  |  |  |  |
|  |  |  |  |
|  |  |  |  |

|  |  |  |  |
|--|--|--|--|
|  |  |  |  |
|  |  |  |  |
|  |  |  |  |
|  |  |  |  |

|         |         |         |         |
|---------|---------|---------|---------|
| SUBJECT | SUBJECT | SUBJECT | SUBJECT |

# WEEK #

| | SUBJECT | SUBJECT | SUBJECT |
|---|---|---|---|
| **MONDAY** | | | |
| **TUESDAY** | | | |
| **WEDNESDAY** | | | |
| **THURSDAY** | | | |
| **FRIDAY** | | | |

| SUBJECT | SUBJECT | SUBJECT | SUBJECT |
|---|---|---|---|
|  |  |  |  |
|  |  |  |  |
|  |  |  |  |
|  |  |  |  |
|  |  |  |  |
| SUBJECT | SUBJECT | SUBJECT | SUBJECT |

# WEEK #

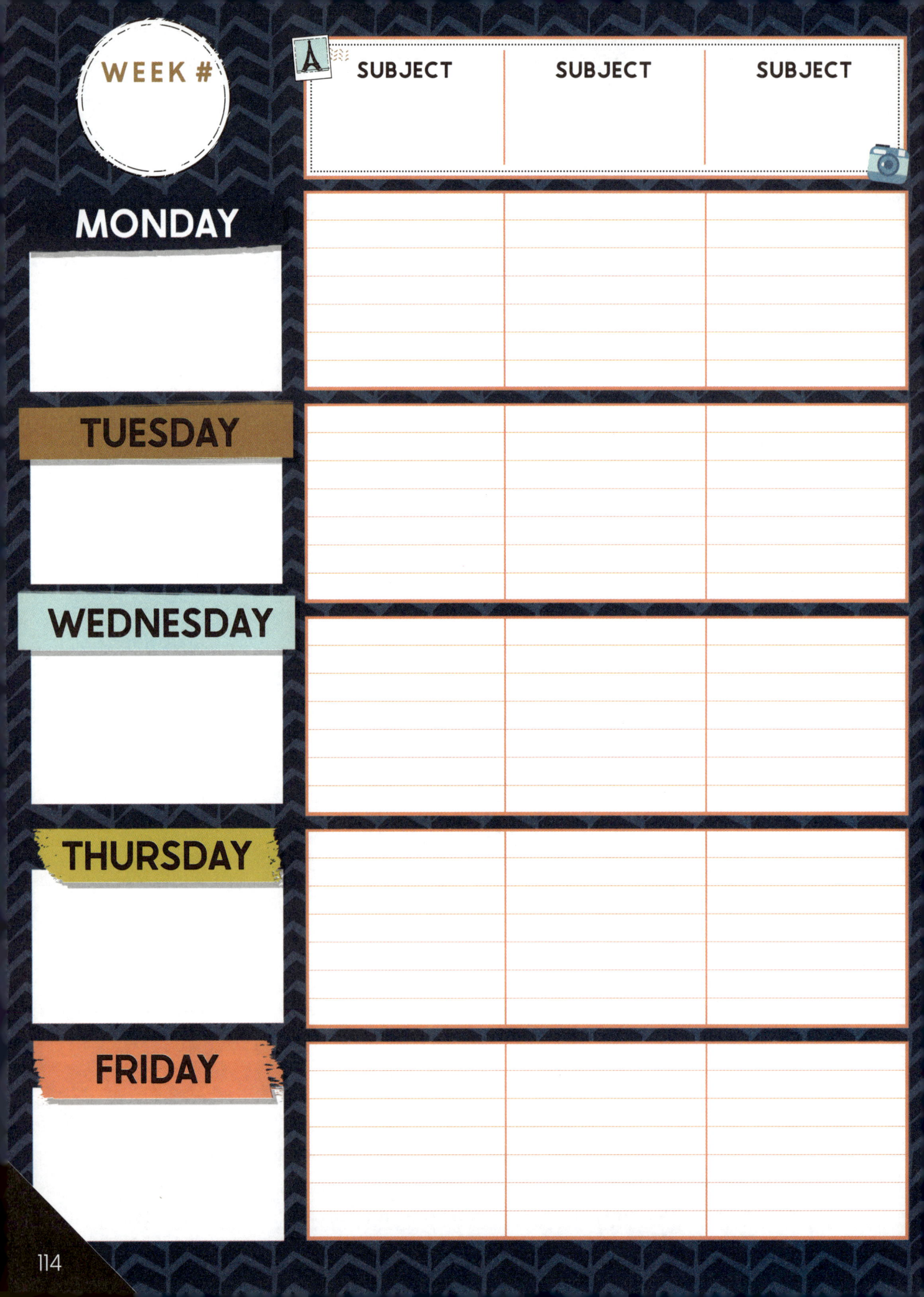

|  | SUBJECT | SUBJECT | SUBJECT |
|---|---|---|---|
| **MONDAY** | | | |
| **TUESDAY** | | | |
| **WEDNESDAY** | | | |
| **THURSDAY** | | | |
| **FRIDAY** | | | |

| SUBJECT | SUBJECT | SUBJECT | SUBJECT |
|---------|---------|---------|---------|
|         |         |         |         |
|         |         |         |         |
|         |         |         |         |
|         |         |         |         |
|         |         |         |         |

# FLIGHT MO-11 CHECKLIST

## name

**FLIGHT M0-11 CHECKLIST**

name

PSST! CUT THIS SECTION OFF SO YOU ONLY HAVE TO WRITE YOUR CLASS LIST ONCE.

FLIGHT M0-11
CHECKLIST

name

# CHECKLIST

**name**

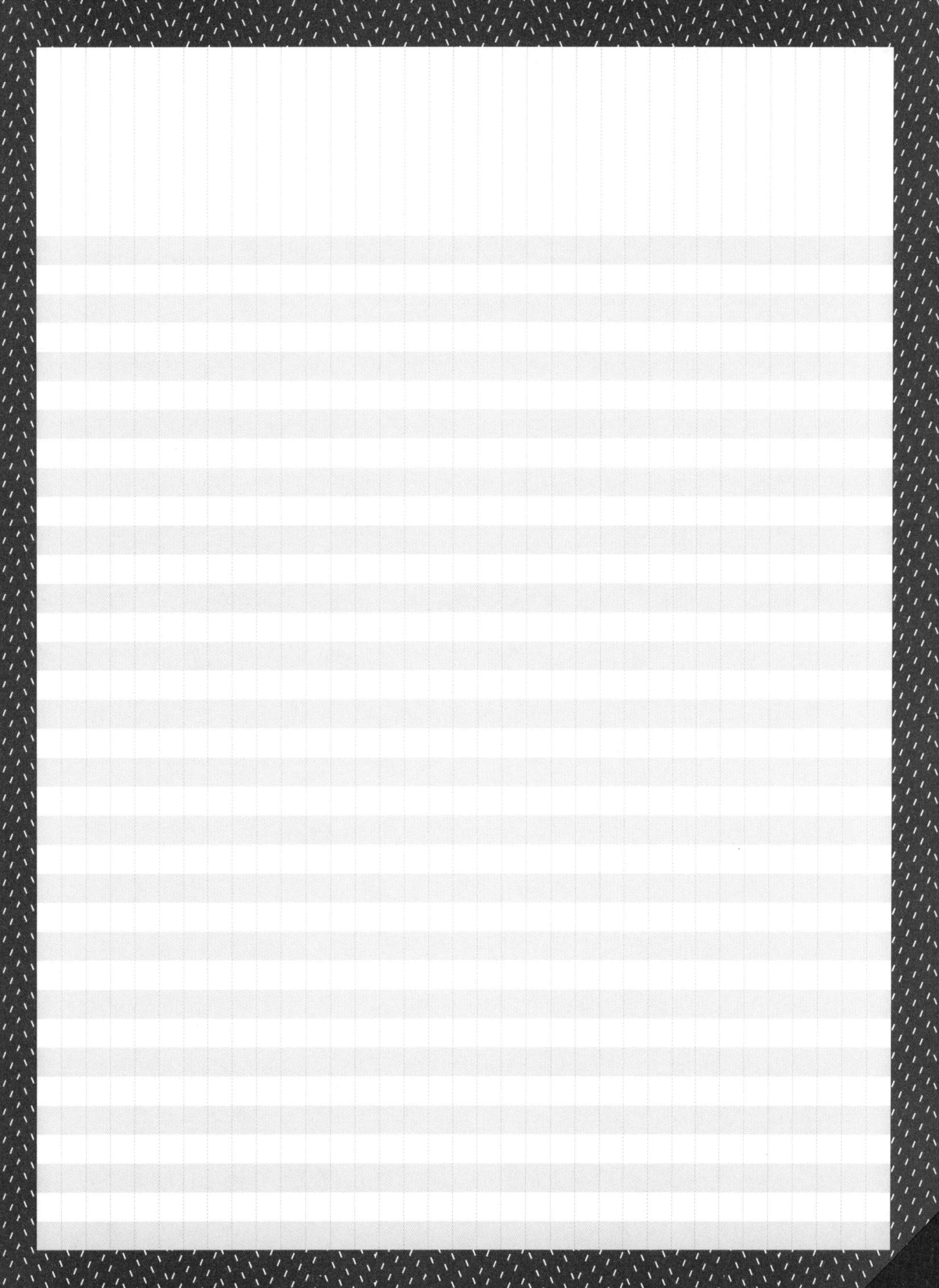

**FLIGHT MO-11 CHECKLIST**

name

125

FLIGHT M0-11
CHECKLIST

name

# ADVENTURES FILL YOUR HEAD & HEART.

BON VOYAGE

LESSON PLANS | LESSON PLANS | CHECKLISTS | CHECKLISTS

JUNE | JUNE | MAY | MAY | APRIL | APRIL | MARCH | MARCH

FEBRUARY | FEBRUARY | JANUARY | JANUARY | DECEMBER | DECEMBER | NOVEMBER | NOVEMBER

OCTOBER | OCTOBER | SEPTEMBER | SEPTEMBER | AUGUST | AUGUST | JULY | JULY

| CONFERENCES | CONFERENCES | STAFF MEETING | STAFF MEETING | PROFESSIONAL DEV. |
| CONFERENCES | CONFERENCES | STAFF MEETING | STAFF MEETING | |
| ASSEMBLY | EARLY RELEASE | EARLY RELEASE | EARLY RELEASE | PROFESSIONAL DEV. |
| ASSEMBLY | EARLY RELEASE | EARLY RELEASE | EARLY RELEASE | |
| HOLIDAY | HOLIDAY | HOLIDAY | TESTING | PROFESSIONAL DEV. |
| HOLIDAY | HOLIDAY | HOLIDAY | TESTING | |
| NO SCHOOL | NO SCHOOL | NO SCHOOL | IEP MEETING | |
| NO SCHOOL | NO SCHOOL | NO SCHOOL | IEP MEETING | |
| REPORT CARDS | REPORT CARDS | REPORT CARDS | REPORT CARDS | |

| * | * | FIELD TRIP | REMEMBER! | REMEMBER! |
| | | FIELD TRIP | REMEMBER! | REMEMBER! |
| * | * | FIELD TRIP | MUST DO! | MUST DO! |
| | | | MUST DO! | MUST DO! |
| | | PROGRESS REPORTS | DO THIS! | DO THIS! |
| * | * | PROGRESS REPORTS | DO THIS! | DO THIS! |
| | | PROGRESS REPORTS | DUE: | DUE: |
| | | PROGRESS REPORTS | DUE: | DUE: |
| | | | DUE: | DUE: |